Traveling the South-Central States

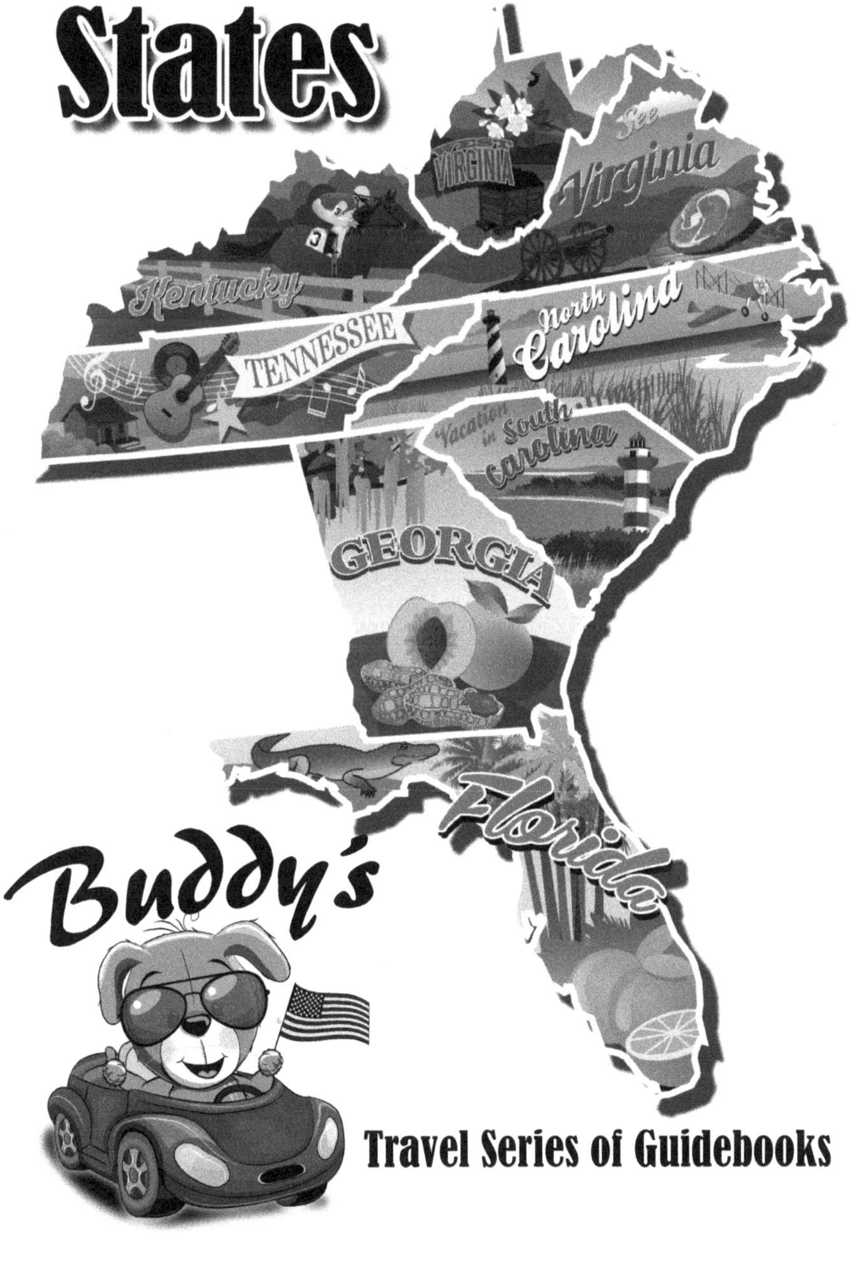

Kentucky
West Virginia
See Virginia
Tennessee
North Carolina
Vacation in South Carolina
Georgia
Florida

Buddy's

Travel Series of Guidebooks

Barringer Publishing, Naples, Florida
www.barringerpublishing.com

Cover, graphics, layout design by Linda Duider

ISBN: 978-1-7352525-5-1

Library of Congress Cataloging-in-Publication Data
Buddy's Travel Series of Guidebooks:
Traveling the South Central States

Printed in U.S.A.

DEDICATION

Before proceeding with this travel guidebook, I wish to thank my wife for our fifty-five years and for her support of all my many projects in life, and more recently this travel guidebook. I also am appreciative of her being my lifelong, traveling partner. Thanks for the memories! There have been so many trips together to so many destinations that we stopped counting years ago. Together, we have addressed each trip as yet another lifetime experience. The experience of writing this book, during perhaps the most diffcult period of our lifetimes, has been an exuberating divergence from these several dark days for both of us! I couldn't have gotten through so many wonderful experiences, or even this particularly challenging endeavor, without her.

WEST VIRGINIA
Louisville
Lexington
KENTUCKY
VIRGINIA
Winston-Salem
Knoxville
NORTH CAROLINA
Chattanooga
Charlotte
Huntsville
SOUTH CAROLINA
Atlanta
GEORGIA
Savannah
Tallahassee
Jacksonville
FLORIDA
Orlando
Tampa
Port Saint Lucie
Cape Coral
Miami

TABLE OF CONTENTS

CREDITS AND PERMISSION FOR PICTURES

(chronological order used)

Silver Springs Tour Boat	Silver Springs State Park	Daniel LeBlanc
Southern Belle River Boat	The Southern Belle River Boat	Jon Reinert
Old Fort Harrod State Park	Kentucky Department of Parks	David Coleman
My Old Kentucky Dinner Train	R.J. Corman Railroad Group, LLC	Benny Getting
Ark Encounter	Answers in Genesis	Tiffany Winkler
Horses (Kentucky Horse Park)	Animals Network	Royalty Free—Website
Exhibition Coal Mine—Beckley, WV	City of Beckley, WV	Leslie L. Baker
Cass Scenic Railroad—Cass, WV	MSR&LHA	Robert Hoke
Savannah, GA, Riverfront—Restaurants	Island Communications	Liz Shumake
Castillo de San Marco	National Monument—Royalty Free	Mary Sims
Historic McDowell County, WV Courthouse	Welch, WV	Jason Grubb
Welch, WV Attractions	Welch, WV	Jason Grubb
Welch Market	Welch, WV	Jason Grubb
Sterling Drive-in	Welch, WV	Jason Grubb

INTRODUCTION

For our family, taking a leisure trip has proven to be a memorable experience. Personal feelings of a traveler, at any one time, depend upon many variables that include: being lost, weather, roads, confusing directions, traffic, road conditions, tiredness, and disrespectful drivers.

However, those negative feelings can be significantly diminished by spending time on trip planning! Everyone should annually re-engage themselves with their families by taking a trip within some type of both time and money budgets. Over the course of our fifty-five years of marriage, taking almost annual, adventure-filled trips—first, as newlyweds; second, with our three children; third, with ourselves as empty-nesters; and fourth, and finally, as seniors we created fond memories for our entire family. Somehow, somewhere, sometime, or someway we have managed to take trips, as we have succeeded in visiting all fifty states, with the lone exception of Hawaii. God willing, we hope to continue these always anticipatory, challenging, and adventurous sojourns for many more years. This difficult year of 2020 just might enable us to continue our traveling, depending upon the course of pandemic conditions, which could hamper length, distance, budgets, attractions, restaurants, hotels, and methods. Nevertheless, taking a trip—again with much planning—just might be the salve for the "stay-at-home" predicament that we all hope may soon be in our pasts.

One of my all-time favorite TV advertisements was a Disney-featured, small boy displaying his excitement by giggling his feelings, with a simple explanation: "I'm going to Disney World today!" He was so full of anticipation and excitement, with his silly, little "hee-hees" that any viewer couldn't help but immediately share some of his giddy excitement. Perhaps you might remember that particular commercial several years ago. But, don't we all feel relieved, if not that frivolous, when heading out for a well-needed period of "R & R?" However, the exciting experience of traveling almost always results in a more relaxed feeling for having taken the trip in the first place! Like the little boy going to Disney World, all of us should wean our progeny on the lifetime art of traveling!

Traveling for me started as a small boy who was fortunate that my maternal grandparents took me every weekend on little day trips around our Northwestern Pennsylvania Allegheny Mountains at first, then prolonged those experiences more and more as I grew older. Stretching out our trips depended upon how I could better comprehend and enjoy longer trips. I can still recall one of my earliest such trips that was a short drive from my hometown, through the lovely Allegheny Mountains' forests, then over dirt backroads through scenic Hearts Content, and finally to the Sheffield, PA garbage dump. Yup, you read it right—a garbage dump! Today, I still chuckle at that choice. But as strange spending a few Friday nights on such a trip might initially seem, the adventure came to fruition when a family of black bears, including three, devilish little cubs, appeared from a dense forest to scrounge the new dumping for an evening's free meal. There were about a dozen cars, similar to an outside movie theater, filling the sizable parking lot to see this wilderness experience live and for free!

Watching those undisciplined, cute, baby cubs and their stern, mama black bear supervise them comprised an engaging first nature experience. Fortunately the three of us repeated that Friday night episode, until the cubs grew up—much like watching a TV serial progress on a weekly basis. Just a short travel to a neighboring, small town introduced me to what became our own conceived "zoo!"

Another pleasurable recollection ensued through frequent Saturday night short trips to Hearts Content's local forests in the dark to spotlight deer. Grandma, Grandpa and myself all became extremely attentive and focused at becoming keen watchers and counters of deer eyes that shine in the dark, with the aid of large spotlights attached to Grandma's car. These regular backroads tours were certainly more fun and entertaining than staying home watching *Bonanza* on TV. Now I wish I could go back in time and thank Grandma and

Grandpa for those "beginning life" travel experiences!

In 1958, my maternal grandpa took me on the most exciting trip of my adolescent years: one that will forever remain as my most steadfast teenaged memory! You see, Grandpa was born in Kansas City, MO, in 1890, and in his senior years—my mid-teens—he earnestly wanted to place headstones on his parents' graves while the trip was still possible with his advancing arthritis! However, years later, he admitted that really his motivation came out of his knowledge that soon I would be moving on in life to college and beyond; Our time together was becoming shorter as both his senior and my adolescent years were as they say, "growing long in the tooth."

Aware of my avocation for baseball, especially "my" New York Yankees, and that combined with his lifelong love for trains, Grandpa wanted me to experience a train trip, before train travel became completely outdated. In the summer of 1958, Grandpa conjured up a very unique experience. It certainly resulted in one we both could enjoy together, notwithstanding, the huge variance in our ages, preferences, and mobility. So, off we went, two best friends, departing initially on a bus, from my hometown, to Erie, PA, where we boarded the New York Central Railroad's *Metroliner,* for a relatively short trip to Cleveland, OH. While staying at the Auditorium Hotel, we got to see the star-loaded, 1950s Yankees play the former World Champion (1954) Indians two nights in a row. Wow, what excitement this was for a Yankee fanatic teenager: Mickey Mantle, Yogi Berra, Whitey Ford and the entire team!

Then, the next day, we boarded the same *Metroliner* to Chicago. After Grandpa's nap, we took a sightseeing tour from the lobby of our Conrad Hilton Hotel. That night, we took my first taxicab to the baseball game between the Orioles and White Sox. Afternoons while Grandpa took his daily, arthritis-driven one-hour nap, this teenager got to meander around the area near our hotel, usually looking for arcades to play pinball games! The next day we took the Burlington & Northwestern train up to Milwaukee and back to see Warren Spahn and the Braves play Stan Musial and his Cardinals.

Early on a Sunday morning, we took the dream train trip of that era, the Santa Fe *Chieftain*—all day riding in the special dome car to our ultimate goal of Kansas City, MO. That day's train experience was highlighted by this geography lover's first crossing of the Mississippi River! While in Kansas City, we took some local, bus trips to visit first the monument company nearest to the cemetery, a Phillips 66 oil refinery, in nearby Kansas City, KS, and then a full day north fifty miles to St. Joseph, MO to see both the Pony Express Headquarters and Jesse James' historic home. Particularly impressive for a young kid was seeing the exact, well-marked spot, in the living room, where the deadly bullet from Robert Ford's Colt 45 had pierced the wall. (Years later, I took my wife to see the same two landmarks, as I wished to share memories of that very special childhood experience with her, through a repeat visit.)

Our "baseball" trip continued in Kansas City's old, now razed Memorial Stadium ballpark, with two games between the Kansas City (then) A's and the visiting Washington (then) Senators. But the "dream" highlight was staying in the same Kansas City, MO, Muehlebach Hotel with my Yankees, whom we also saw play two more games. My "nap-time" pleasures consisted of procuring autographs in the 1958 *Yankees Yearbook* of every New York Yankee player, as well as being lucky to sit on a counter stool beside legendary Yankee Manager Casey Stengel. As we shared time over lunch, Mr. Stengel picked up the ticket for his new friend from Pennsylvania! My cherished, fully autographed yearbook I thought would become a lifetime treasure.

That all surprisingly ended when I departed for college. Much to my chagrin, my distraught mother cleaned out my room without notice to me of what memorabilia she would discard in my absence!

Our "dream trip" wound down with another train ride to St. Louis, for our last ballgame between the Dodgers and Cards (Musial again, but opposing Sandy Koufax!) The next two days were comprised of sightseeing and another three trains—first to Cincinnati, then to Cleveland, and finally to Erie—before the final bus trip home—all in fourteen days. That trip was so monumental for me as a youth, that I still cherish the longhand-scribbled log I kept, during that eventful (and highly memorable) trip. That log, from my first true "trip," is a precious reminder of time well spent with a very loving Grandpa! The special log still resides in my home office drawer!

Just getting it out and reading it—usually on my birthdays—still causes a warm feeling of remembrance today!

Memories from trips with your children can't be substituted as time really does fly!

As the years have gone by, our entire family of five has all grown together. We traveled with our kids during our summers and some winters too. Together, we successfully toured every national park, amusement park, most major museums, and most major league ballparks. Often, we used our old, 1985, chevy custom van that we all coveted as the "family car!"

Not surprisingly, as an *aficionado* for major league sports (plus a staunch traveler)—mainly major league baseball, I have been so lucky in my lifetime to have experienced the sports travelers' thrill of professional baseball, football, hockey, and basketball in eighty-two different indoor and outdoor stadiums, throughout the USA. During my years, cities like Pittsburgh, Philadelphia, and Cincinnati have each built three stadiums.

Pittsburgh alone is a good example of time frames, as I have been to four sports venues, including Forbes Field, then Three Rivers Stadium, and recently beautiful PNC Park—my very favorite professional sports stadium—in addition to the Igloo for hockey.

So, I urge all Americans to take regular trips while their family can still enjoy together their favored places, experiences, and activities. Travel, as you can see by my lifetime of traveling, can and should be an anticipated, adventurous, exciting, and most memorable experience. Travel can especially be a prescription for family bonding, sharing quality time, and cherishing family togetherness—

whether it's for one day, a few "getaway" days, two weeks, or whatever would be appeasing and affordable for each family. There's no time like the present, as our lives go by so quickly. So, act now parents, take the whole family somewhere in the coming summer!

Enough memories of travel in my lifetime. Now, it's on to these very special travel destinations that are covered in this guidebook. All families could use this guidebook somewhat as a gateway, so that families can leave their homes and enjoy the many recommended and described travel destinations.

Now, let's begin with a quiz—answers to the following questions, relevant to some of the top attractions covered in this book, will be revealed as their destinations appear.

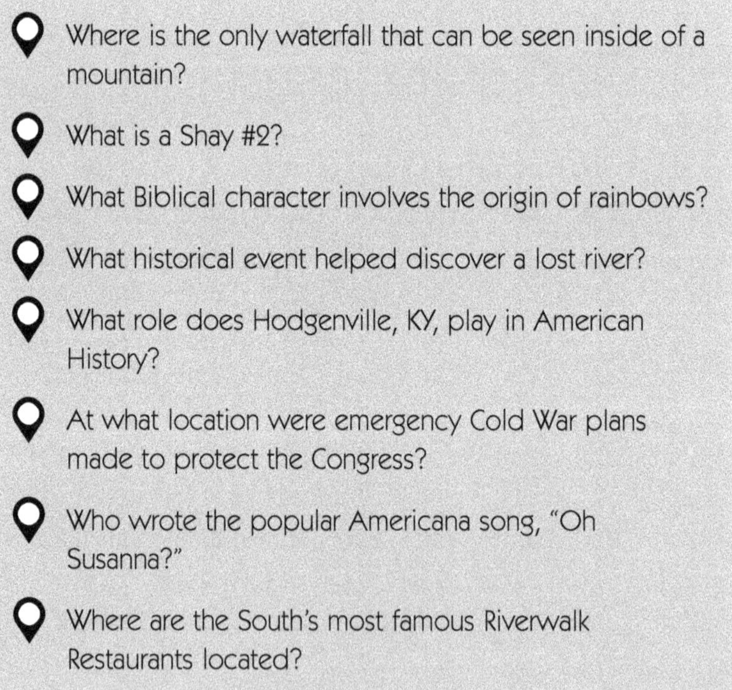

- Where is the only waterfall that can be seen inside of a mountain?
- What is a Shay #2?
- What Biblical character involves the origin of rainbows?
- What historical event helped discover a lost river?
- What role does Hodgenville, KY, play in American History?
- At what location were emergency Cold War plans made to protect the Congress?
- Who wrote the popular Americana song, "Oh Susanna?"
- Where are the South's most famous Riverwalk Restaurants located?

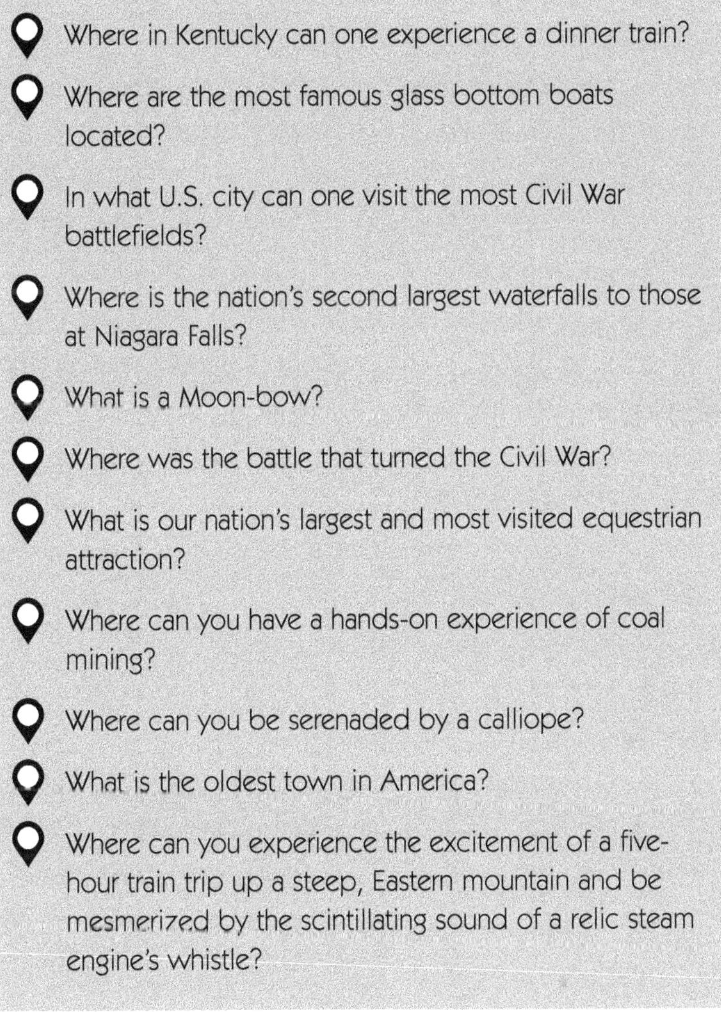

- Where in Kentucky can one experience a dinner train?
- Where are the most famous glass bottom boats located?
- In what U.S. city can one visit the most Civil War battlefields?
- Where is the nation's second largest waterfalls to those at Niagara Falls?
- What is a Moon-bow?
- Where was the battle that turned the Civil War?
- What is our nation's largest and most visited equestrian attraction?
- Where can you have a hands-on experience of coal mining?
- Where can you be serenaded by a calliope?
- What is the oldest town in America?
- Where can you experience the excitement of a five-hour train trip up a steep, Eastern mountain and be mesmerized by the scintillating sound of a relic steam engine's whistle?

Answers to all of the above questions—and perhaps many more—await as you read and use this guidebook to aid in planning for your upcoming family vacations!

We all know that each of our fifty states has a motto. What is geographically interesting is to learn all of those mottos, but even more fun, is visiting the various states in order to decipher why those nicknames were chosen to respectively label each state! Can you identify the eight states' mottos covered in this book, by matching them up with their nicknames: "The Peach State;" "The Bluegrass State;" "The Volunteer State;" "The Mountaineer State;" "The Sunshine State;" "The State For Lovers;" "The Palmetto State;" and "The Tarheel State?" Answers come later in this book!

However, before assessing the book's over thirty recommended adventures, please sample two such experiences, at your earliest opportunity on each of their respective internet websites. First is the website for *Stephen Foster Songs*, as an opportunity to recall, sing-along, and identify popular songs attributed to this man's legacy as "The Father of Americana Music." Second is the website for *Steam Locomotives*—Cass, WV. You will be happy that you availed yourselves of these first hand experiences, especially as a precursor to the balance of this guidebook.

Please note that I have not included prices, availability, or lists and locations of hotels in this guidebook.

Weather is a keen issue in traveling, especially with an itinerary of outside venues like most of those covered in this guidebook.

By researching weather forecasts beforehand, better preparations, packing, and planning may just make the trip a better experience.

Getting your travel vehicle ready is of prime importance. Air in the tires, small repairs of key issues, clean oil, and a full tank of gas are all important to getting your trip off to a positive beginning!

Another key issue, for animal lovers like us, was boarding our German Shepard. It is incumbent on each of us to investigate any new boarding kennels as part of our trip planning. Unacceptable experiences with boarding kennels can wreck an entire trip. It is imperative to take time to ensure that your pet will receive the proper care in your absence! Boarding the day before, may allow for an earlier and less hectic departure.

Depending upon your place of residence, perhaps you can reduce driving distances, improve access to this guidebook's listed travel attractions, increase your convenience factor, reduce expenses of your planned travels, and better monitor your time frames—all by starting trips from your own initiation points. Please refer to the maps in this book. The first map entwines the entire eight states covered in this tour book. Also, please note that the overall trip constitutes a roughly-planned circle. Depending upon your individual choices of all, many, or just some attractions, you could plan your stops through the different north, east, south, or west accesses to the circle. For more detail by state, following that regional map are individual maps of the eight states. Below is a graphic displaying pertinent data for each direction, the nearest city to listed attractions, and interchanges of U.S. Interstate Highways, major U.S. highways, and scenic parkways which conjoin either near or through that city.

NORTH

Cincinnati, OH

WEST

Louisville, KY

Bowling Green, KY

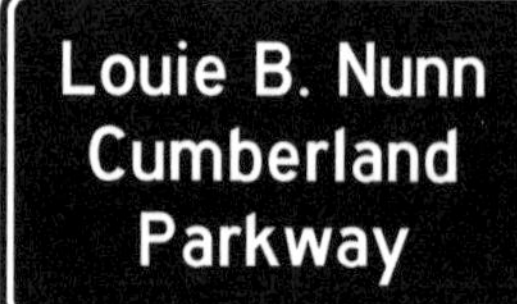

EAST

Lexington, VA

SOUTH

Lake City, FL

This travel guidebook encompasses a driving trip taken in June 2019 to all eight southeastern states over an eleven-day period! All attractions in this travel guidebook have been personally experienced—some several times. If you choose to replicate the June 2019 trip (which excluded stops in Atlanta and Savannah—other than drive-throughs), it would entail driving 2,992 miles—mostly interstate highways. However, a large amount (27%) of those miles resulted from necessarily traversing the entire long state of Florida twice, from bottom to top and back—about 402 miles up and 411 back or a total of 813, just in Florida. Therefore, should your home be closer to the track of that trip, total mileage for non-SW Florida residents should be more like 2,000 miles! That could be accomplished by only averaging a very doable 181 miles per day!

Please take note that two-night stopovers were necessary for three nights: Chattanooga, TN, Bardstown, KY and Lexington, VA. Perhaps you might choose to parcel the listed attractions to better match time, money, and favorites from the many listed destinations in this travel guidebook. The regional map, included at the outset of this book, certainly confirms that these adjoining and centralized eight, Mid-South states represent a combined geographical area that is highly accessible to a large percentage of Americans! Huge population centers may be only one full or even partial driving day away!

Happy traveling wherever or whatever you choose for your vacations or even day excursions!

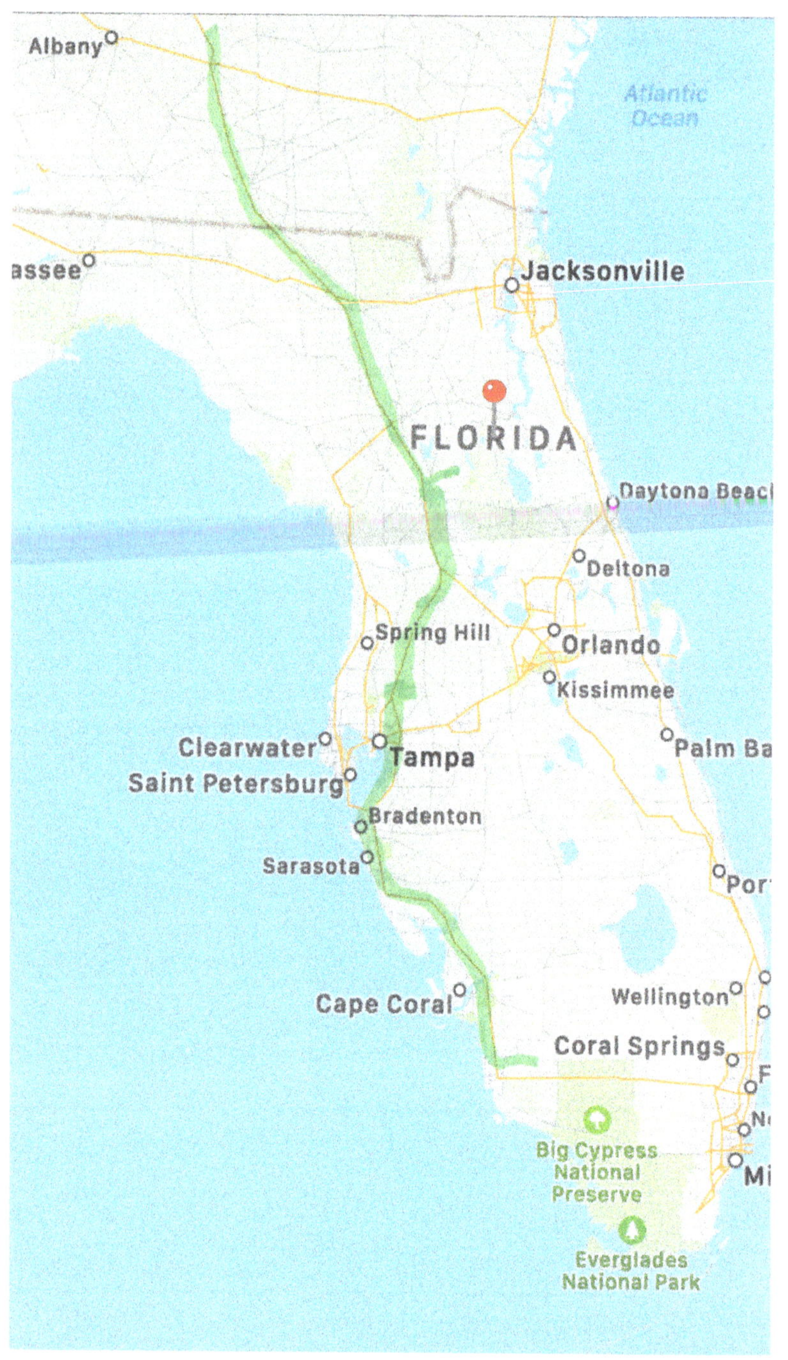
Albany
Atlantic Ocean
assee
Jacksonville
FLORIDA
Daytona Beac
Deltona
Spring Hill
Orlando
Kissimmee
Clearwater
Tampa
Palm Ba
Saint Petersburg
Bradenton
Sarasota
Por
Cape Coral
Wellington
Coral Springs
Big Cypress National Preserve
Everglades National Park
Mi

CHAPTER ONE

DESTINATION
TIFTON, GA 463 MILES

The drive north on I-75 from extreme SW Florida up "The Sunshine State" is not very scenic until the Ocala area, which is about 463 miles. Unfortunately, taking the only acceptable route of I-75N leaves no closeness to any Gulf of Mexico views. The only scenic views are restricted to the Charlotte Harbor Bridge near Port Charlotte. Driving comprises all flat ground over either two or four lanes. Traffic usually does not become congested, until the four Sarasota exits. From there, across I-4 and around Tampa, the highway can easily become clogged. Past the Tampa vicinity, the topography remarkably changes to rolling hills and lakes, and is more scenic to the Georgia state line. There are only three rest stops along the way.

Ocala, FL

The distance to Ocala is 277 miles. Access to Ocala from the south is Exit 350 on I-75N, which leads to State Road 200. Turn right initially onto ST200, then turn right, east on State Road 40E.

A recommended lunch stop traveling north on I-75 is in Ocala, at a tasty and quick favorite of the locals named Richards Place. Richard's Place, located in the Historic District, is a home cooking emporium with mouth-watering sandwiches, daily specials, and other traditional lunches. Their hot roast beef and turkey sandwiches are tops. Richard's Place is on the right, the last building of the "Historic" complex, located at 316 Silver Springs Road, on the corner.

Spending some time in Ocala is a great refresher, especially after a long drive! We always enjoy Richards, as his welcoming wife has adapted well to running the breakfast and lunch only restaurant. Ocala is located in the middle of the nation's second largest equestrian area, with the largest being the Lexington, KY, area.

Ocala has an interesting history that provides some insight also into the history of Florida. Archaeological excavations date to its

beginnings back around 6500 B.C.! In early historic times, the Timacua inhabited the area which was then called "Ocale," or "Ocali." The site was originally a major Timacua village; the chiefdom dated around the 16th century. The name Timacua is believed to mean "Big Hammock" in their language. Spaniard Hernando de Soto discovered Ocale in 1539, during an exploration of the area, however history has recorded that the Timacua made an attack that eventually scuttled the newly established settlement.

Several European countries tried to claim permanency, until the late eighteenth and early nineteenth centuries, when the Creek people, along with other Native Americans and some freed African American slaves populated the area. Eventually the Seminole Tribe claimed the area. Europeans returned to colonize the area with control changing from Spain to Great Britain and back again, until 1821, when the U.S. acquired the territory of Florida. In 1827, the U.S. Army built Fort King near modern day Ocala in an effort to better manage the growth of white settlers in the area. The Fort was a key center during the Second Seminole War, and later served, in 1844, as Marion County's first courthouse. The early town of Ocala was officially established in 1849, acceding to the courthouse site. The area around Ocala is known as the "Kingdom of the Sun."

Citrus production became the main industry, until the Great Freeze of 1894-1895. The arrival of rail service, in 1881, greatly enhanced the commerce of the area and established Florida's commercial reputation for produce. After a fire destroyed the city in 1883, the city was rebuilt with brick, granite, and steel rather than wood. The newly built city became known as "The Brick City." The first thoroughbred horse farms in Florida arrived in 1943, making Ocala then the center of the equestrian industry. The most famous horse from Ocala was *Affirmed*, which won the 1978 Triple Crown of horse racing! Presently, Ocala's population is over 250,000. Its charmed Historic District is a well-kept warm reminder of Ocala's past.

Silver Springs Glass Bottom Boats

In June 2019, we finally completed an item on our "bucket list," by extending our luncheon stopover to visit the key, famed Ocala attraction. Located further east from downtown on State Road 40E—about five miles on the right—is Silver Springs State Park. There resides one of the wonders of the world—Silver Springs Glass Bottom Boats. Years ago, as an adolescent, I had a "Viewmaster," which at that time was perhaps the best educational offering for famed places to visit. From that beginning, a must-see visit ultimately became almost mandatory.

SILVER SPRINGS GLASS BOTTOM BOATS

Silver Springs offers guided boat tours in boats with glass bottoms, which enables the uniqueness of viewing life underwater in the springs-driven, gorgeous lake. The facility is lovely, with its well-maintained historic walkway entry past several shops, primarily for food, ice cream, and other snacks. After an engaging three-block stroll, we reached the boat ride's lake to view the enchanting scene of the highly specialized boats. Tickets are sold at a very economic price. Tour guide/pilots take travelers on perhaps the most unique and also one of the most interesting boat tours available in our entire nation. They do not allow reservations, but the wait that weekday afternoon was only fifteen minutes, as the previous boat completed its journey. It is compelling how beautiful the multi-colored spring waters are, especially from the side-seated benches that are smooth, and conform comfortably to the body, and which rest on the narrow, wooden floors, just in front of the boat's glass bottoms. The guide/pilot drives the boat, and narrates for the approximately forty-five minute to one hour trip around the lake. The boats cannot accommodate wheelchairs or pets, other than service animals, for which you must display proper identifications. These special, custom boats showcase the crystal clear springs and highlights the nature-inhabited underwater life. Visitors can see into the depth of the water, which is about ten feet deep, and view wildlife as well as other interesting images. The guide points out peculiar vegetation, as well as historical and cultural artifacts left in the waters over the years. Of particular notice were Native American artifacts, a rowboat brought by early Spanish soldiers, and movie props from the plethora of Hollywood movies over years past that have been produced at Silver Springs. All of these have remained for many years beneath the cool, fresh, spring waters. All in all, it was worth waiting much of a lifetime to see this iconic, picturesque site and its unique boats and tour.

Tifton, GA

From Ocala, take I-75N, after driving nine miles from the Springs, on US 27 west. From Ocala to the Georgia State line is 120 miles. Tifton, GA is 43 miles north from the Georgia State line on I-75N. The Hampton Inn and a plentiful supply of other hotels are just a right turn at I-75N's exit 61, onto US 82E, then immediately on the right. For quiet enhancements with hotels on busy interstates, always reserve an opposite side room.

Although we prefer the more dependable **Hampton Inns,** this one is particularly a favorite, since it also offers a free, tasty dinner, called their "potato dinner." But, so many other foods and deserts make this more than filling for the night's "all-included" meal. In fact, this night's stay was completely free, since we had earned, with sufficient points, a free room, plus the next morning, also, a free and more nutritional breakfast—a win, win, win!

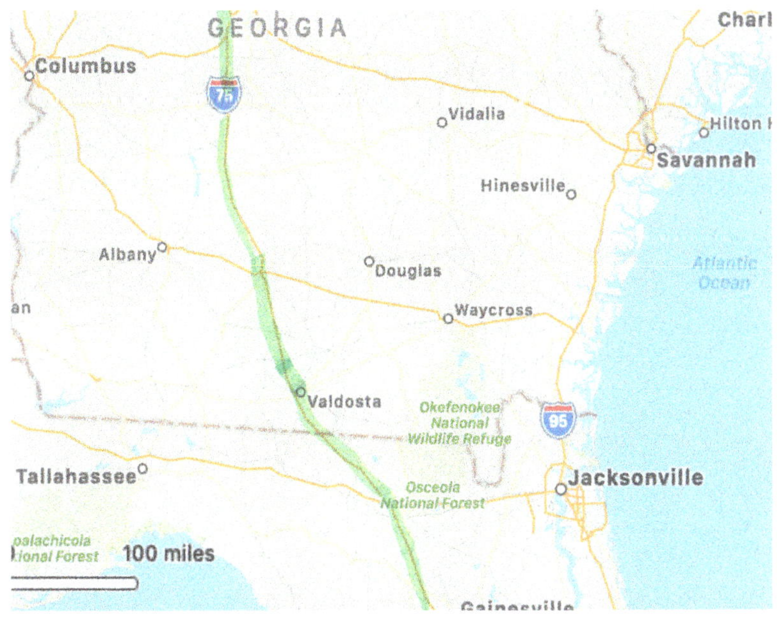

Louisville
Lexington
Owensboro
KENTUCKY
Bowling Green
Nashville
TENNESSEE
Knoxville
Great Smoky Mountains National Park
Chattanooga
Huntsville
Roswell
Johns Creek
Atlanta

CHAPTER TWO

DESTINATION
CHATTANOOGA, TN 226 MILES

Our daily travel goal comprises leaving as early as possible, after a good breakfast, as we target 8:30 a.m. for desired departures. I-95N through Georgia can also be as tedious as parts of Florida, but the traffic is usually steadier without much congestion until the Macon, GA, area. From Macon north to Atlanta the roads get more than challenging! Atlanta is 163 miles from Tifton.

Atlanta, GA

Although on the June 2019 trip, we did not stopover in Atlanta, there are many special attractions in Atlanta, the Capital of the South, and the state capital of "The Peach State!" We have visited Atlanta dozens of times, but more recently several times over our nearly twenty retirement years. A key issue with Atlanta is traffic—24/7! Visitors need to ready their maps and appoint a navigator! You must know beforehand, your destination, what highways to use, and the exact numbers of the routes necessary to traverse through Atlanta's many interstate highways in order to survive difficult Atlanta!

Atlanta is the nation's ninth largest city, with a population of 5.6 million. For families with younger children, even teenagers, Atlanta deserves some family time due to its often confusing network of fun opportunities for kids too! Atlanta is a comparably new city to others its size "up North." Organized in 1837 when a new railroad station was built to tie Atlanta with Chattanooga, Atlanta began its rapid development due to that 1837 historical, commerce-building milestone. However, on July 22, 1864, the Union Army, led by Ulysses Grant, burned the developing new city to the ground. That horrific event ushered the end to the Civil War. Following the destruction, Atlanta began rebuilding as today it has become the "Crossroads of the South!"

Georgia Aquarium

A visit to Atlanta could encompass a week of attractions, depending upon available time and personal preferences. Quite possibly the best "bang for your bucks," as well as most interesting, might be the impressive Georgia Aquarium, located downtown, at 22 Baker Street. This massive building houses seven separate exhibit galleries featuring four whale sharks, with the largest reaching twenty-four feet long. The aquarium holds ten million gallons of water and is solely an inside experience. The attraction will necessitate minimally two to three hours. Garage parking is available on site.

World of Coca-Cola

Secondly, another well-attended downtown attraction, adjacent to the Aquarium, is "The World of Coca-Cola," at 121 Baker Street. Another large, indoor experience, with several dedicated, differentially themed units, the museum highlights the history of the "coke" drink as well as several other equally fun and educational opportunities, most of which are dedicated to their motto of "the real thing!" They like to humorously note that their highly secretive formula for the drink is not included in the visit. The tour begins in the "Coca-Cola Loft" where the history of the famous drink can be traced by visitors; plus "The Loft" introduces visitors to other company products available for consumption. Make sure you don't miss the "Taste It" area, which enables visitors to taste with a paper cup 100 diverse drinks from around the world. All you have to do is grab a paper cup and start sipping—slurp, slurp, slurp! Upstairs, watching TV commercials from the past constitutes a nostalgic trip down memory lane, in the Perfect Pause Theater. Those old enough to recall these classic ads, and preferentially their theme songs, can sing along with the tune to: "I'd Like To Buy The World A Coke," sung to the old tune of "I'd Like To Teach The World to Sing In Perfect Harmony." You'd better hang onto your seat in the museum's 4-D theater as it spins with breakneck speed to find a discovery of what makes a Coke taste like a Coke!

Six Flags

Perhaps spending an afternoon at Six Flags of Atlanta amusement park might help ease the kid's pent-up energy from traveling! This fun treat is located at 275 Riverside Parkway, which is best approached off the western loop of I-285, also known as the circle route around Atlanta. It is just west on I-20W, after exiting "the loop," at I-20's exit 10/51. This particular amusement park is not so big that it would take days to see, and is not so small that it wouldn't entertain the kids for minimally half a day! It is probably the most perfect amusement for half a day kid's entertainment!

Stone Mountain

A rural, symbolic, geographic wonder is Stone Mountain, located eighteen miles east of downtown. It is best approached off the eastern side of the I-285 loop, and then east on I-20E; Exit 39B eight miles to US 78, and finally just at Exit 8. Since we visited several years ago, this special, one-of-a-kind, magnanimous attraction has expanded past "just" Stone Mountain" into a 3,200-acre park with over a dozen specific attractions, historical and natural sights, and an expansive, natural woodlands, with many nature trails. Stone Mountain itself is a massive, bowl-shaped, granite formation that formed beneath the earth's surface some 300 million years ago. Perhaps the most popular tourist adventure at Stone Mountain is the Summit Skyride. Selectively for history buffs is the Historic Square, a self-guiding compound of 18th and 19th century houses, and other old-time buildings which have been re-located from around the state.

The above recommended activities can take two or three days, but visitors with specific interests can easily spend one whole day enjoying the "Capital of the South!"

Kennesaw Mountain National Battlefield Park

After leaving downtown Atlanta, "double" ensure that you use only I-75N towards Chattanooga, TN. A must stop is north of Atlanta twenty-one miles on I-75N to Marietta, GA. Then getting off I-75N Exit 269, take US 120 West two and one half miles northeast, turn left /south on US Old 41, and proceed four miles south, through some picturesque mountains, to The Kennesaw Mountain National Battlefield Park. This second-largest Civil War battlefield (Gettysburg is the largest) is more than just another must-see for select, history *aficionados.* Although the entire park is on hilly terrain, the parking lot is an easy walk across the street to the park's headquarters/souvenir store. This parking lot can get quite crowded quickly, but it is also close to the paved road that proceeds almost straight up the mountain to another parking lot that is halfway to the top. Able-bodied visitors can either walk or drive the quarter of a mile paved upswing. This historic battlefield had a key role along with Chattanooga's Lookout Mountain in accelerating the end of the Civil War. The further walkway to the top is dirt, crowded, and almost too steep for most seniors. The halfway parking lot has a very good visibility to Atlanta, just twenty miles or so to the south. However, advancing minimally just to this upper parking lot leads to a better understanding of Civil War strategy that paid off with Sherman's "Run Through Atlanta" that virtually ended the war.

In June 1864, General Joseph E. Johnston's Confederate Army rushed to needlessly take control of Kennesaw Mountain as a strictly strategic view of the North's primary target—Atlanta. Northern Army with General

William Tecumseh Sherman and his troops cleverly skirted the mountain and proceeded straight and unopposed towards the city of Atlanta. This forced Johnston and his troops to disastrously withdraw from the mountain and attempt to reposition and beat Sherman to Atlanta. Sherman, therefore, forced the Confederates to abandon their secured positions at Kennesaw which quickly resulted in a losing and ultimately failing effort to take a defensive position to protect Atlanta. As such, Sherman outmaneuvered Johnston to end the war. This war-ending story, and now historically, pivotal, National Park exposes one of the war's greatest strategic battles. The Park Rangers, at their headquarters log cabin, describe the battle, oversee the many history books, and sell souvenirs and snacks to usually well-attended crowds due to the park's close proximity to Atlanta.

The drive north, from Kennesaw and north I-75N, suddenly loses its "boring drive," as it soon becomes a winding, interstate highway through the scenic Appalachian Mountains all the way to Chattanooga, which itself is surrounded by beautiful mountains. The seventy-four-mile drive to Chattanooga on I-75N is certainly picturesque.

If you are hungry, the **Farm Fresh** diner, just off I-75 in Calhoun, GA, offers fresh, tasty, home cooked lunches! To find the diner, take the only side road for Calhoun off I-75N west for one mile, as the diner is on the right! When you reach Tennessee you soon experience why Tennessee is called "The Volunteer State!"

KENNESAW MOUNTAIN NATIONAL BATTLEFIELD PARK

CHAPTER THREE

DESTINATION
CHATTANOOGA, TN 45 MILES
(TWO NIGHTS' STAY ON THE JUNE 2019 TRIP)

Chattanooga, TN

Chattanooga, TN, is one of the most progressively modern and growing cities in America, with perhaps the nation's most up to date infrastructure system of expressways in its sized category. Chattanooga is truly a busy crossroads, with three super highways converging on Chattanooga: I-75 connecting Atlanta, GA, south and Knoxville, TN, north; I-24 connects with Nashville, TN, west and I-59 connects with Birmingham, AL, south. As the fourth largest city in Tennessee, Chattanooga had a population of 550,000 at the last census. The city has rightfully earned the esteemed title of "Scenic City."

Chattanooga was founded in 1776, by the Cherokee Indians Tribe and its then chief, Dragging Canoe. The Native American era ended abruptly in 1838, with the disastrous "Trail of Tears"—the properly named U.S. Government's Department of Interior's project designed to relocate the Indians from the North Carolina-Tennessee area on foot all the way to Oklahoma. That calamitous, U.S. Government directive nearly annihilated the entire tribe, took thousands of lives, and caused horrific suffering—all the way driven by U.S. Calvary troops, for the entire, thousand mile distance.

Cherokee, NC has a summer outdoor production entitled "Unto These Hills," in a new amphitheater at its new location, at the southern tip of The Great Smokey Mountains National Park, just off route 441. The historical drama is designed for children and families, as it teaches the theme of Cherokee legends. It opens every May and closes in mid August, since mostly college students portray parts in the professional production.

We saw the show in OK, but not yet in NC.

Lookout Mountain National Battlefield Park

The area's location was key to the ultimate results of the Civil War, as three separate, but very definitive, battlefields that surround Chattanooga remain huge tourist destinations. The city is steeped in history!

The first key battle occurred on Lookout Mountain. Today, it is a National Military Park, complete with a self-guided tour and U.S. Interior Department operated museum. However, this prestigious battle allowed the Confederates a temporary victory, as they chased the Union Army away, for a short period of time. The main trail on top of the mountain near the National Military Park's museum and headquarters allows a view of the city and far beyond from this highest point in the region. The trail continues, with an optional hike, partway down the very, steep front of Lookout Mountain. This adventure allows one a moment's pause for how steep the digression actually appears. No doubt that much of a drop is much more severe than any of the other battlefields such as Gettysburg. To imagine any army marching up that mountain front, in the face of enemy fire, evokes a

horrific and shocking feeling. However, after U.S. Army General Ulysses Grant refurbished his troops so quickly following the earlier set-back, an extremely risky climb back up that very mountain is exactly what led the Union Army to a winning string of victories. In almost rapid succession, the Union Army took that well-earned victory from Lookout Mountain, and continued that progress to nearby Chickamauga, and then to nearby Missionary Ridge. These three, Chattanooga area string of victories continued at Kennesaw Mountain in Georgia and finally, Atlanta, which, when all combined, led to a rather quick end to the Civil War. Chattanooga provides a historian's delight with all of its history stories, from the "Trail of Tears" to the three, pivotal, Civil War battlefields.

In recent history, Chattanooga has earned three distinctive national awards for "livability." The reasoning for such honors and why the city has been so continuously praised is rather easy to understand with just one visit!

The Hampton Inn

Hamilton Place is both centrally located and easily approached—right off I-75N at Exit 4A. After exiting I-75, the route is just a quick right and quick left up the steep hill leading to the impressively situated hotel at the top. The view all around the area from the hotel is magnificent. Perhaps, this Hampton Inn has one of the most picturesque views in the U.S. The hotel is just a short drive to most places like Chattanooga's restored downtown, historic and charming Lookout Mountain, and home-spun suburbs like Soggy Daisy. Shopping is nearby—just down the mountain, across the street.

Restaurants like our favorite **Bonefish Grill** are just down the street and across the farther side of Hamilton Place Mall.

Lookout Mountain

The place to start a visit to Chattanooga is no doubt Lookout Mountain. Directions are easily followed, with the local tourist map offered to all hotel guests, at the "Chattanooga Choo Choo" downtown, and other locales. Lookout Mountain is both towering and statuesque, as it has truly become a natural landmark for the entire Southeast Tennessee region. It can be easily identified from all over the Chattanooga area. Driving up Lookout Mountain is curvy and steep, but directions on expressways are easy to follow. Once on top of the famed mountain, you traverse to the front visage point of Lookout Mountain National Battlefield Park. Views are spectacularly breathtaking, especially on a clear and sunny day. The locals rightfully boast that on a clear day you can see into seven far off states! The city, the Tennessee River, and major expressways are almost as if you were in a helicopter. Parking is plentiful, the walkways are paved, wide, and offer plentiful, historical data almost regularly on markers, as you proceed around the trail that circumnavigates the top.

Walking the equivalent of no more than three blocks, the park trails are easy for most visitors. Two museums are directly across the street from the parking lot. The National Battlefield Park Historical Museum has more to offer than the adjacent private one, including a short film of the battle. Leaving the mountain, a sizable area of the mountain top behind the National Park comprises one of the nicest residential, suburban developments in the entire Chattanooga area.

Incline Railway and Rock City

Also, near the same area on Lookout Mountain, there are two, additional attractions. First, the main road passes the Incline Railway which climbs from bottom to top, with equally spectacular views. Then towards the rear of the mountain, Rock City allows self-guided tours and also spectacular views from a different viewpoint. One combined, discounted ticket can be used for these two plus Ruby Falls.

Ruby Falls

Once down the mountain, Scenic Drive can be picked up and then travel halfway around to the front of the mountain for an enjoyable and amazing visit to Ruby Falls, located at 1720 South Scenic Drive. Exploring the unique caverns of Ruby Falls, senior-level guides take you on in depth, extended tours of this nature's wonder. Ruby Falls is the nation's tallest and deepest underground waterfall that is open to the public. Discovered in 1928, a team of excavators found a breath-taking waterfall deep within Lookout Mountain. Founder Leo Lambert named the fall after his wife, Ruby, and opened the attraction to the public in 1929. Today, Ruby Falls welcomes over half a million visitors annually. The key feature of the experience is the light shining through the falls, which makes a beautiful and colorful impression with visitors.

Back down and off of Lookout Mountain, and located on the northern side of downtown, are two, excellent, tourist attractions: the Tennessee Aquarium and the Southern Belle Riverboat tour.

The Tennessee Aquarium

The Tennessee Aquarium opened in 1992 and is located at One Broad Street. Directions include tolerating the many one-way streets downtown, by proceeding on the same street that comes off of Lookout Mountain, then making a left turn onto Market Street, which runs north and south, then turn West onto West Aquarium Way, and finally proceed right/

north again, for one short block—then onto Broad Street. The two tall buildings which comprise the aquarium stand out in the city scape. This top, regional, tourist attraction presents in its Tennessee River Gallery "The Story of Water," which traces the path of water from the nearby Tennessee River to its merger with the Ohio River, then to the Mississippi River, and finally into the Gulf of Mexico—quite an educational geography lesson! Other areas include "Tropical Cove," "Turtles of the World," and separately, its "Ocean Gallery." In addition, it covers the other key rivers of the entire world.

In the "Ocean Gallery" separate "cams" include: Stingray Bay, Penguins Rock, Secret Reef, Boneless Beauties like octopuses, and Undersea Cavern. Animals include otters, turtles, frogs, freshwater fish, sharks, penguins, butterflies, and jelly fish. Tickets are available without reservations. Plentiful parking is available in the parking garage, in off-street lots, or on the streets.

Southern Belle Riverboat Trip

Just two blocks to the north and then west, and on the riverfront, is the Southern Belle Riverboat. The river wheeler is at 151 Riverfront parkway, Pier 2. Its tour offers a ninety-minute, wheeler boat ride that is excellently narrated, and also offers the experience of an open-air, refreshing, Tennessee River tour. The highlights include constantly passing scenic views of the entire area, including a different approach of the stately, downtown's views, the many bridges that cross the Tennessee River, Lookout Mountain, and north shore suburbs. Photographers have a field day! Reservations are suggested, as some days the boat tour is overbooked.

SOUTHERN BELLE RIVERBOAT

The tour comprises an up and down river trip on the historic Tennessee River. The surprising conclusion entertains visitors with a seldom found calliope!

There is the choice of a lunch meat meal, for an additional fee. After the boat ride, and if lunch is still desired, then the downtown, **Big River Grill** is a good choice, with excellent service and tasty sandwiches—dinners too, if you are around downtown at dinner hour!

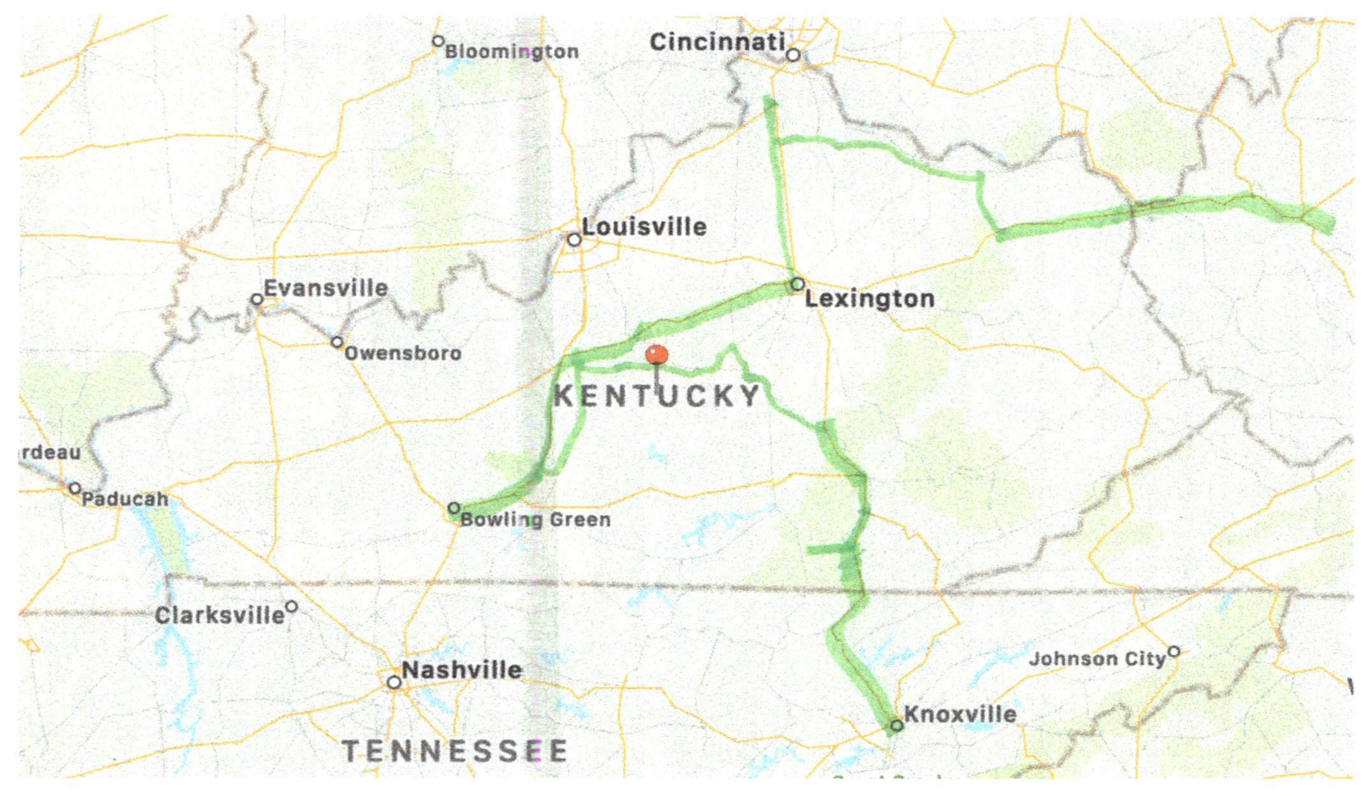

Bloomington
Cincinnati
Louisville
Evansville
Lexington
Owensboro
KENTUCKY
Paducah
Bowling Green
Clarksville
Johnson City
Nashville
Knoxville
TENNESSEE

CHAPTER FOUR

DESTINATION
CORBIN, KY 197 MILES

After leaving favorite destination, Chattanooga, one must wonder what lies ahead that is more attractive, more beautiful, and more enjoyable than SE Tennessee? The answer is undoubtedly that the 197 mile drive up I-75 from Chattanooga, TN, to Corbin, KY is the most scenic part of the entire length of US I-75—which covers its north-south length from Miami, Florida, to Sault St. Marie, Ontario, in Canada. Our goal of Corbin, KY, is located in the extreme rural SE corner of Kentucky, and just west of Appalachia.

The beauty of the "Blue Grass State" of Kentucky is readily notable. The four-lane highway skirts the Great Smokey Mountains National Park, and the topography is the very same as within that park! I-75 in this region is majestically mountainous, scenic, and requires the highest level of attention to survive driving through the constant bevy of commercial trailer-trucks. Passing trucks when necessary is challenging, but doable with the assistance of the mostly wide median that distances the north-bound from the south-bound lanes. The key mystery has been why I-75 seems to end with a "T," when it reaches I-40, which requires a right turn onto I-40E, and proceeds through the heart of Knoxville, TN. The two interstates conjoin for about twelve miles through Knoxville, TN, until I-75N separates and turns north towards Kentucky. Actually the section of I-75 from Knoxville to Corbin is even more picturesque, as the scenery reflects that of the adjacent Smokies!"

Cumberland Falls

Approximately ten miles inside of Kentucky, highway State 90 west crosses I-95, as the direction signs are clearly marked for Cumberland Falls. The "Niagara of the South" is about twelve miles west. The Cumberland Falls State Resort Park is a lovely place to spend the night, if you admire a good rural, quiet, and fun retreat, with a tasty dining reputation. Taking pictures of the seasonal, colorful, beautiful "Moon-bow" that embraces the huge waterfalls is a once in a lifetime experience, since the phenomenon is not found anywhere else in the Western Hemisphere! When you arrive at the falls, the parking lot is upstream. Anxious visitors, selectively fond of waterfalls in general, must take a short walk on the paved trail, which parallels the rapidly falling waters of the

Cumberland River, just before the waters reach the precipice of the falls.

The falls, as wide as Niagara's Goat Island Falls, is a wall of water falling sixty feet into a boulder-strewn gorge, complete with a whispering mist that kisses the face and, at night shines that magical "Moon-bow." The "Moon-bow" is visible just a few days each month, and always on a clear night, under the full moon. Pictures are captivating and wondrous when it exhibits its fullest brightness. The walking path is paved, has a porch-like viewing stand, and a "closeness" opportunity to stand within a few feet of the falling water to experience the mist. The falls are 125 feet wide, as the curtain of falling water is dramatic either by day or night.

The area is a natural favorite of watersports *aficionados*. Rafting, swimming, canoeing, and fishing, with a license, are popular sports for visitors. As much as the spectacular setting surrounding the falls is impressive, the historic Dupont Lodge, built of massive hemlock beams and knotty pine, holds a magical view of the entire Cumberland River Valley. Although we enjoyed a night's stay at the Dupont Lodge once, we chose the Hampton Inn for an easier departure the next morning, expecting another long day. The Hampton Inn is twenty-five miles north on I-75 and then west onto State 25, just off the highway and beautifully tucked into the mountain behind the hotel.

Also, a scrumptious breakfast awaits just a "stone's throw" across the access road from a Cracker Barrel! For dinner, the Old Town Grill, east on State 25 into Corbin, was excellent and a bastion for locals.

Corbin, KY, isn't that far from another landmark tourist site—Cumberland Gap State Park, although it is just a little too far away, unless a full day is available. As a result, it becomes somewhat out of the way due to the curvy forty miles through Appalachia over difficult roads from Corbin. However, it certainly belongs on any "bucket list" for future adventures. It took an entire day to both drive to the Gap, and drive up the steep, surrounding mountains, and to study local history and geography in that unique, three, state area where Ohio, Kentucky, and Virginia come together. The view from those mountain tops and down into the historic gap is deep and quite memorable.

Corbin, KY

Corbin, KY, lies halfway between Knoxville, TN, and Lexington, KY, on I-75. Its population in 2010 was 7,304. The town, with its shops, restaurants, and other businesses, is on the eastern side of I-75.

Corbin, Kentucky's history began around 1885 as a settlement named Lynn Camp Station

and their first post office was called Cummins, for community founder Nelson Cummins. It was found in state records that both of the names had otherwise been previously recorded, so Postmaster James Eaton was asked to choose another name for the settlement. He chose instead Corbin for the Reverend James Corbin Floyd, a local minister. The town was incorporated under that name in 1905.

Because Corbin suffered a race riot, in late 1919, the town has suffered a negative label, with a troubled racial past. The story recalls that a white mob forced nearly all the town's 200 black residents onto a freight train bound for anywhere out of town. That action was followed by a sundown town policy, until around 1990. That "dark" event was the subject of a 1991 documentary entitled *Trouble Behind*.

CHAPTER FIVE

DESTINATION
BARDSTOWN, KY 162 MILES

Berea, KY

Berea, KY, is north up I-75 for sixty miles. Berea is a popular travel target for its art festivals, historic restaurants, and buildings. The town is home to liberal college, Berea College.

Berea's population at the last census was 13,501. It is one of the fastest growing towns in the state, having increased by 27.4% since 2000. Its name traces from the Bible, which lists Beroea as a province in Asia Minor that is mentioned in the "Acts of the Apostles,

17:10"—new Bibles are slightly different. The Bible proceeds to document that its Jewish citizens were more receptive to the messages of the Apostles, but also had obeyed the prophet Isaiah by searching the Scriptures daily to gut-check their behavior, according to "Isaiah 8:20." The town was formally incorporated in 1890.

Berea is an easily adaptable, small town with very friendly citizens, including the students at the college. Berea College was founded in 1955, with a very special platform that still exists today—free tuition, room, and board to students who qualify with both good grades and a need for financial aid. Also, they accept only those students living in nearby Appalachia.

Log House Craft Gallery

The students also must work for the college on its beautiful, rustic campus. The Log House Craft Gallery is located on Estill (US 25) & Center Streets, on the college's campus. The Log House is both the college crafts' retail store as well as the home of arts, crafts, and other similar homemade products made by local students and a few other adult artists living in Appalachia. The roomy, attractively decorated, and refurbished former house is filled with unique and charming weavings, wood-crafted items, brooms, ceramics, and wrought iron products for sale to visitors. Their quality is excellent!

Kentucky Artisan Center

Just outside of Berea, and just off exit 77E on I-75N, is the Kentucky Artisan Center, located at 200 Artisan Way. This modern facility is chuck full of the state's finest, artisan, homemade products that are similar to those of the students at the college.

For sale items include Kentucky-made arts, crafts, music, literature, and foods.

Weekly demonstrations and a cafe offering regional specialties for sandwiches, light meals, or snacks are available.

In retrospect, though, upon leaving both times we visited, we wondered why the duplicity of artisan pros and collegians, just down the street from each other in the whole, good-sized, State of Kentucky? It just doesn't seem fair, to the fledgling college students.

Danville, KY—The Red Rooster Cafe

Heading next to Danville, KY, the route begins by backtracking two miles south on I-75 and then west on State

Roads 21 & 954, over difficult to drive, very rural roads, up and down, around and around; thirty-nine miles through rolling, bluegrass country all the way to Danville, KY.

Quite surprisingly and very hungry, we stopped for lunch at the **Red Rooster Cafe**. The **Red Rooster,** which is located at 118 East Main Street, is this small town's best restaurant. Parking is limited. The best we could find, was a spot on the busy highway, right outside the front door. The place was full of locals; who are also its regular, if not daily, customers. We were again surprised by the daily special for this home cooking hot spot with an offering of a "Manhattan Beef" sandwich. Having never before heard of such a name for a meal, we quickly learned that it was the most tender and very yummiest, open-faced, roast beef sandwich, with mashed potatoes, that we have ever experienced. This is a must place for us, if we ever are in the "neighborhood" again! The restaurant is very clean, roomy, quite aged, but still well-kept, cleverly and attractively decorated, and designed like a refurbished one-hundred-year-old emporium should look like. Resting right on the main highway, it was filled with home-spun friendly staff and clients. We were treated as though we ourselves lived in their small town.

OLD FORT HARROD STATE PARK

After a truly scrumptious, and very filling (shame on us) lunch, we proceeded north on State Road 33 the twelve miles to Harrodsburg to see Old Fort Harrod State Park. The historic and impressively restored citadel encompasses fifteen acres, centered by the closed in, log-fenced old fort. This landmark fort is fronted by a small, country, white, majestically-steepled, log cabin church that is honored to have hosted the marriage of Abraham Lincoln's parents—Thomas and Nancy Hanks Lincoln. The reconstructed fort contains several log structures which represent various aspects of military frontier life, including a militia blockhouse, a family blockhouse, several cabins demonstrating pioneer life, a blab school, a minister's cabin, and the leader's cabin.

The Mansion Museum is a Greek Revival home that contains American Civil War artifacts, a McIntosh gun collection, paintings, documents, music collections, Abraham Lincoln memorabilia, and Native American artifacts. Four senior volunteers were onsite and dressed in period clothing, while exhibiting and employing live demonstrations of fashioning frontier era household utensils and hunting weapons. The very outgoing, informative, and educative male volunteer was making a one-shot rifle that he sells for income. The personable, talented, and home-spun female was demonstrating rug weaving on a huge old-fashioned weaver's loom. She also had a very impressive collection of her hand-stitched, women's clothing. A third volunteer female was tending the vegetable garden, with many pieces ready for a plentiful harvest. The fourth volunteer was a very engaging female who was the ticket taker, as well as local informant on destinations, routes, and various nearby tourism activities. Not anticipating such wealth of learning, history, and knowledgeable exhibitors conjoined into a very enjoyable and much appreciated atmosphere, we spent a somewhat prolonged adventure at the old fort. Selectively, the opportunities to spend personal time with its very pleasant volunteers resulted in one of the best historical stops on our entire trip.

Shaker Village

Another nearby, frontier museum, just east of Harrodsburg, seven miles on US 68, is the Shaker Village of Pleasant Hill. It was founded in 1805 and remains the nation's largest, restored Shaker village. Shakers are celibate members of a communal religious sect that began in the late 1800s in England. Today, the village comprises an outdoor history museum, preserving thirty-four original buildings on 3,000 acres to include streams, forests, and native prairies. More than one dozen of the buildings are available for visitation. With some structures dating from 1809, some of those reflect Shaker norms of simplicity and utility. The stoned Centre Family Dwelling contains Shaker furniture and many artifacts. Costumed interpreters portray and describe Shaker society's distinct way of life, as if it were happening yesteryear. Artisans demonstrate such crafts as broom-making and woodworking. Activities throughout the property include hands-on changing history displays, forty miles of horseback riding and biking trails, a farm experience with petting areas and chicken roundups, organic gardens where visitors can sow seeds, and wagon and hayrides. The paddle wheel riverboat offers one-hour trips on the Kentucky River. Allow four hours minimum.

Shaker Village has justifiably earned the prestigious AAA rating of "GEM," so add this attraction to your "bucket list."

Abraham Lincoln's Homestead

The route to Bardstown, KY, proceeds west on State Road 152 about twenty-five miles to Springfield, KY. From Springfield, another anticipatory stop is with a right turn up very rural (one lane) State 528 to Abraham Lincoln's Homestead. This well-publicized homestead side trip was most disappointing, as the boarded up, faded and peeling home, plus visible evidence of damaged property, all combined to make our side-trip a total sham. Even their historical sign in front had been irreparably damaged beyond use. The five-mile return to State Road 152, with the right turn west again restored the approach of fifteen miles to Bardstown.

Bardstown, KY

The Bardstown Hampton Inn's location allows close reach to all the many Bardstown attractions, and is located at 985 Chambers Boulevard.

Breakfasts are either free at a Hampton Inn or home-cooked at Bardstown's highly recommended eatery—**Mama's**. Bardstown's breakfast hot spot is West Stephen Foster Avenue, which is also known as US 62 west. Dinner at the well-recommended **BJ's Bar & Restaurant,** located about three miles down State Road 245—Bardstown's "circle-route"—was excellent.

Bardstown is a great tourist town, which is quickly evident when handed the Visitors Guide Area Map that is filled with dozens of attractions, restaurants, motels, six distilleries and bourbon plants and markets, and a very friendly Welcome Center. The latest population in 2010 was 11,700, but a good guesstimate might reveal that their "in season" population soars to three or four times that level. Yet, proceeding through the tourist traffic seems easier than at other similar American tourism cities. The center-piece of Bardstown is My Old Kentucky Home State Park, Picnic Area, and Campground.

Historically, the city is named after the pioneering Bard brothers. David Bard obtained a 1,000-acre land grant in 1785, from Governor Patrick Henry, in what then comprised Jefferson County, Virginia. William Bard surveyed and platted the town. Originally chartered as Baird's Town in 1788, the town also has been known as "Beardstown" and "Beards Town."

Bardstown was first settled by European Americans in 1780. Named county seat of then Nelson County, Virginia, in 1784, the town was formally established in 1788.

Finally, it was incorporated in the Kentucky State Assembly in 1838. Mirroring the westward migration beyond the "Blue Ridge," after the Revolutionary War, Bardstown became the center of Roman Catholicism west of the Appalachians. That expansion resulted in pioneering into the western frontier of the then farthest reaches of the U.S.! The Catholic Diocese of Bardstown was established in 1808 to serve all Catholics between the Appalachians and the Mississippi River. Historically this divided the Diocese of Baltimore, established in 1789, which originated geographically as the

only Roman Catholic Diocese in the Colonial Era. As a comparison and representation of the growth of Catholicism in the nation, there are now forty-four dioceses and archdioceses in the same ten state grouping today—a representation of the expansion of the Catholic religion in America.

The Bardstown cathedral is named the Basilica of Saint Joseph Proto-Cathedral, since in 1841, the seat of the Diocese was transferred to the nearby, larger, river town and port of Louisville, KY.

The Old Talbott Tavern, built in 1779, and located just off the Courthouse Square in the center of Bardstown, constitutes a landmark of the city's history. Amongst the many notable Americans who have entered this relic include Abraham Lincoln and Daniel Boone. Bullet holes shot by outlaw Jesse James are notable in the upstairs wall.

My Old Kentucky Home State Park

Most evenings, from early June to mid-August at the outdoor J. Dan Talbott Amphitheatre, in My Old Kentucky Home State Park, the electrifying three-hour musical—thematically named as the Stephen Foster Story, is presented. The entertainment is top notch, with seasoned singers and dancers performing nearly all of Stephen Foster's iconic "Americana songs," for a most entertaining and reminiscent night's engagement. The singers harmonize the tunes, with Hollywood-level, orchestral accompaniment, while the dancers perform many skits that aspire to choreography found only on Broadway. The uniforms and gowns are lovely to behold, charming in a way that embellishes the entire production, and perfectly adaptable for each skit's segment of the program. The evening's entertainment successfully evolves into a most pleasant and lasting memory for the appreciative crowd of live theater *aficionados*. The outdoor auditorium is so colossal that even a twenty-minute intermission seems insufficient to gaze over the evening's program, take a short walk, or seek out a cool drink. Reservations are recommended as the 1,450-seat venue is sold out for most performances, especially as the weather warms. It is recommended, too, that visitors call ahead for the schedule. This musical drama undeniably captures the spirit of Foster's idolized works.

The composer's life is portrayed through his memorable musical accomplishments, with his highly popular American compositions. The most memorable tunes include: "Camptown Races," "Oh! Susanna," "Jeannie With The Light Brown Hair," "Hard Times Come Again No More," "Old Folks At Home," "Way down upon the Swanee River . . . ," "Old Black Joe," "Beautiful Dreamer," and "My Old Kentucky Home." In 1928, the latter song was formally adopted into the official state song of Kentucky! These songs are so special that perhaps most Americans can sing, if not all of the tunes, at least a few bars from memory.

Stephen Collins Foster (July 4, 1826 – January 13, 1864) became honored as "The Father of Americana Music." As an Americana songwriter of over 200 songs, many of his songs remain popular today. Once a visitor enters this magnificent outdoor facility, with its historical background and huge stage, those songs will resonate for years if not a complete lifetime! We are not alone in saying that we have been honored to have witnessed this excellent production three different times in our lifetime. It was interesting to note that when we were there, one elderly man sitting just in front of us said that he had missed only one presentation, since the beginning of the show many years ago.

Foster was born in 1826 into a family with nine siblings, in Pittsburgh, PA. After attending three Pennsylvania academies (prep schools), he attended Jefferson College (now Washington & Jefferson College in Washington, PA), where he taught himself to play the clarinet, violin, guitar, flute, and piano. While his tuition was paid, he had little pocket money to spend, so he moved to Cincinnati and became a bookkeeper with his brother's steamship company. During that period, he wrote several of his iconic songs. He returned to Pittsburgh to sign a contract with the Christy Minstrels, when he wrote most of his songs over a twenty-year period, from 1844 to 1864. During that period, he experienced much difficulty getting jobs and pursuing a career in music, since the Foster family did not support the abolition of slavery.

Many of Foster's songs were typical of the highly, popular, blackface, minstrel shows common during his era. He attempted to improve the trending political disenchantment of abolition with more upscale words that he felt might seem more suitable to refined people, instead of the trashy and really offensive words which are found in such songs of that genre. However, in the 1850s he joined-up with an abolitionist leader, and actually, quite surprisingly, wrote an abolitionist play himself. Although many of his songs had Southern modes, he never lived in the South. He actually visited the South only once during his lifetime and that time only for his honeymoon.

Various stories seem to conflict with his tragic ending when he lived four years in New York City, since Foster's brother destroyed records that the brother felt were discrediting; These records have been sealed by the family—preserved but unavailable to the public. There are several plaques regarding his time spent in various locales during his life, but the

only actual memorial is on the University of Pittsburgh (Pitt) campus on Forbes Avenue in the Oakland District of his hometown of Pittsburgh, PA. Allocated adjacent to the famed only U.S. college campus high rise skyscraper building, the Cathedral of Learning, the Stephen Foster Memorial Performing Arts Center is an excellent example of a quality theatre and center for the arts for Pittsburgh. It also holds many of his works and artifacts.

CHAPTER SIX

DESTINATION
BARDSTOWN, KY 216 MILES
(TWO NIGHT STAY OVER)

The route mostly south from Bardstown to Knob Creek Farm, Abraham Lincoln's Boyhood Home, is sixteen miles on US 31E. This well kept, reconstructed, 19th century log cabin on the site where he lived from 1811 to 1816 is located in a lovely, rural, farm area, that is fronted with a well-marked pull off on US 31E. It is maintained and manned daily by the National Park's Department of the Interior. Allow thirty minutes.

View of hills, or knobs, surrounding Knob Creek Farm.

In 1811, the Lincoln family moved ten miles from the Abraham Lincoln Birthplace National Historic Park north to Knob Creek Farm, which itself is seven miles south of Hodgenville, KY. Most history literature has made note of Hodgenville, KY, as Lincoln's birthplace, but that is not entirely true. The Kentucky soil was richer for farming as Lincoln helped his father plant pumpkin seeds on their new farm, which Lincoln testified as among his fondest early memories. There, the boy got his first taste of education in Caleb Hazel's "ABC school," or as Lincoln labelled it, a 'blab school," because of the constant recitation. Lincoln's views on slavery may have been formed at Knob Creek, as Hazel was an outspoken emancipationist, and the Lincolns belonged to an anti-slavery church. Life was better there for the family, but the slavery issue, along with lawsuits over the titles to their farms, induced his father, Thomas, to move to Indiana.

So late in 1816, the Lincolns crossed the Ohio River into Illinois. Thus, the Illinois State motto has since become "The Land of Lincoln," or the land where the child matured into manhood.

ABRAHAM LINCOLN BIRTHPLACE NATIONAL HISTORIC PARK

From Knob Creek Farm to the Abraham Lincoln Birthplace National Historic Park is only ten miles down 31E, and is well marked. Eschewing a biographical history of Abraham Lincoln, since many history books and articles have been written over the years, an "excerpt" from the National Park brochure is perhaps the most complete, yet shorter and most accurate version of what other research can produce, on the subject. More importantly is that the National Park Service has printed in its hand out brochure its best description possible for history buffs. Just walking up the fifty steps—one for each U.S. State—the Kentucky Memorial inspires a "proud American" feeling, but seeing the one room, tiny eighteen-by-sixteen-foot log cabin replica is a wondrous experience in itself. The birth cabin replica has been placed inside the protection of the well-built cement and stone duplicate of the larger version on the Capitol Mall in Washington, D.C. The almost exact replication in Kentucky constitutes an equally impressive experience, especially when considering that a family of four occupied that extremely small frontier homestead for several years. The excerpted National Park rendition is as follows:

Almost 100 years after Thomas Lincoln moved from Sinking Springs Farm, a log cabin originally accepted as the birthplace cabin of Abraham Lincoln was placed in the Memorial Building. While the cabin is old and typical to the area, it is not the original Lincoln cabin. The National Park Service considers it a symbolic cabin.

New York businessman A. W. Dennett purchased the Lincoln farm in 1894 and had the cabin moved to a site near Sinking Springs. But shortly thereafter, it was dismantled and reassembled for exhibition in many cities. In 1905, Robert Collier, the publisher of Collier's Weekly, purchased the farm where Lincoln was born. Collier along with Mark Twain, Samuel Gompers, and others, formed the Lincoln Farm Association in 1906 to preserve Lincoln's birthplace and establish a memorial to the nations's 16th president.

That same year, the group purchased the cabin and raised over $350,000 from 100,000 citizens to build a memorial to house the cabin. President Theodore Roosevelt laid the cornerstone in 1909. In 1911, President William

Howard Taft dedicated the marble and granite memorial, designed by John Russell Pope. The neoclassical structure in a farm setting may seem grandiose for a man who wrote: 'I was born and have ever remained in the most humble walks of life.' But the rough cabin within the memorial dramatizes the basic values that sustained Lincoln as he led the nation through its darkest period.

The memorial and Sinking Springs Farm were established as a national park in 1916 and designated Abraham Lincoln Birthplace National Historic Site in 1959. Abraham Lincoln Boyhood Home at Knob Creek became a unit of Abraham Lincoln Birthplace National Historic Site in 2001. This date marked the culmination of efforts my many individuals and groups, including the Kentucky General Assembly, the Kentucky Heritage Land Conservation Fund Board, the Larue County Fiscal Court, and the National Park Trust, to purchase this historic property from the Howard family, who had operated the site since the 1930's. In 2009 the site was designated a national historic park."—end quote!

Lost River Archaeological Cave

One of America's largest caves is Mammoth Cave National Park. The park is located just off I-65 and just north of Bowling Green, KY. Most visitors today have difficulty obtaining tickets during the busy summer months' vacation period. After an attempt to purchase tickets for our lifetime would-be second visit, we were told by a park employee in their ticket department that unless a visitor is camping onsite within their park, and since no hotels are closer than campers, it is doubtful that tickets remain available. It seems that a percentage of daily tickets are held for 8 a.m. purchase and pick up only on the day of the requested visit. As a result, when we requested two tickets, we could only secure one. This seems an unfair injustice to travelers other than campers! So still desiring to tour a cave while in Kentucky, we chose another nearby cave with a highly interesting story—Lost River Cave, 2818 Nashville Road, Bowling Green, KY.

Lost River Archaeological Cave is in the Central Time Zone, so consideration of that one-hour time difference is mandatory. All time elements of such a visit to this particular cave are one hour earlier than in the Bardstown / Abraham Lincoln memorials' adjoining region.

From the Lincoln Memorial, highway US 83E is seventy miles to I-65 South towards Bowling Green. The rural cave is located off I-65S Exit 20 to 31W (Nashville Road), then on Dishman Lane (Cave Mill Road) head west until reaching the well-marked cave. The cave is part a walking cave but mostly a boat tour. Only reservations are accepted, and the cave temperature is 56 degrees. The trip involves a walk down a steep, paved path to the cave entrance where the guide awaits the group of visitors to board the small tour boat, for the major part of the trip.

The Lost River Cave constitutes the only underground river cave in Kentucky. The dock area contains steel fences with railings to assist with walking a few more even steeper steps lower to the water level. Once seated in the john boat which is propelled by a more powerful tow motor, the guide/pilot narrates a history of the cave as the slow-moving boat approaches an almost scary, steep drop off. Because it is difficult to sight the dam just ahead, passengers begin to fear a coming accident, in which the boat could quickly tumble down several feet into the gravel below the dam. Almost suddenly, the guide yanks the boat around, just before the boat might cascade over the precipice! With that excitement behind us, while motoring back to the same entrance dock to conclude the one-hour tour, the guide explains the history dating back 10,000 years to the Paleo Indians. Also, the cave's history includes that it was once the sight of a 19th century water-powered mill, then was a campsite used by both sides in the Civil War, and then became a hiding place for outlaw Jesse James, and finally a popular 1930's night club.

The unsolved mystery of the cave resulted when visitors seeking the bottom of the cave's depth actually drowned. However, it was of concern for a long period of time that their bodies could not be found due to the cave's swift and peculiarly strong, underground, river current. The mystery went unsolved for years, since the cause of the string of drownings remained hidden and therefore unknown as the strong current is found only at a great depth and far underneath the surface of the cave. The cave does eventually empty outside its interior, but not for the several minutes that it requires for an object/body to travel its swift and deep undercurrent and pass deep under the lava in which the natural cave was made by nature eons ago. A short, nature walk after the boat tour exposes the three "blue holes" where the drowned bodies were removed from the cave. It is important to note that this boat tour is completely safe, since the boat does not enter the deep underwater area which is further downstream and many feet beyond the boat docks. The area where the boat sails is only a few feet deep, and there is no current in the touring area underwater. The trip proved to be a fun, adventurous, somewhat thrilling, and educational experience.

The return to Bardstown is north on I-65 about ninety-five miles to The Blue Grass Parkway, then east to the Bardstown exit. Staying two nights in Bardstown is recommended to enjoy the several described attractions.

My Old Kentucky Dinner Train

To close out the stay in the touristy Bardstown area, a final dinner with **My Old Kentucky Dinner Train** certainly comprises a wonderful last night in a superior town.

MY OLD KENTUCKY DINNER TRAIN

The train depot is on 31E or 602 North 3rd Street, which is the main thoroughfare north and south in Bardstown. The 2 1/2 to 3-hour, thirty-eight-mile round trip is scenic, tasty, and fun as the restored 1940s dining cars are modeled after the snazziest old-time trains of yesteryear. The tour passes through the Bernheim Forest, past the Jim Beam Distillery, and through many rural neighborhoods, before reaching its farthest point. At that place, the train then very interestingly reverses course at an old-fashioned train turn-around system of switches at Limestone Springs. At that point the train began retracing the tracks back to Bardstown. The act of having the engine turn around at the 180 degree switching location constituted a new, fascinating journey for all four of us at our table. The train is pulled by diesel electric engines. The entire experience recaptures the experience of vintage American railroad dining—a seldom available opportunity today.

Reservations are a must, since the gourmet meal offers customers a choice beforehand of five meal type options that include: prime rib, smoked paprika chicken, chimichura pork roast, barbecue shrimp and grits, or vegetarian pasta, with some choices of the dessert included. The meal is prepared in the train station's kitchens and served in route by experienced servers. Each table seats two couples, so that experience itself affords another new and unique opportunity to meet and visit, with two strangers for two and one half hours, which we thought was also fun and adventurous. The dress code is somewhat discriminatingly dressy casual, as it is expected that all guests will dress in accordance with those guidelines. Alcoholic drinks are available. No children under the age of five are permitted. Although some might consider that the dinner train experience may seem quite expensive for two, but since the entire experience is "one of a kind," most on board thought that the experience was definitely worth the expense!

CHAPTER SEVEN

DESTINATION
ASHLAND, KY 290 MILES

After a good breakfast, departing Bardstown, KY, as early as possible will greatly assist in allocating time to take in two major attractions and drive to the next overnight stop in Ashland, KY. The quickest route is to take The Bluegrass Parkway east fifty miles to the Parkway's termination in Lexington, KY. The first few miles on Lexington city streets, while proceeding fifteen miles between the Parkway and I-75N, can be confusing, while navigating over the several side roads required to traverse Lexington. The connecting route is well-marked, with a string of several directional road signs that point the route towards I-75N. However, concentrating closely on the many road signs becomes a challenging task.

Kentucky Horse Park

Once on 1-75 north, proceed about nine miles north of Lexington to the Kentucky Horse Park, which is located off I-75 Exit 120 east, at 4089 Iron Works Pike. Directions to the Park are clearly marked. This highly popular attraction has rightly earned the prestigious AAA rating of "GEM"—an absolute "must" for your "bucket list!"

KENTUCKY HORSE PARK

The history of the world's only equestrian park is about man's relationship with the horse. The park's history is quite an interesting story that covers a period of time just over 200 years, from 1777 to 1978. In 1777, Governor Patrick Henry bestowed a land grant for 9,000

acres to his wealthy brother-in-law, William Christian, as a recompense for Christian's stellar service, in the French and Indian War. Colonel Christian and his family then relocated to Kentucky, in 1785, to settle into a new farm on Beargrass Creek, which is near Louisville. When he was unfortunately killed by Indians in 1786, his daughter, Elizabeth Dickinson, inherited specifically only 3,000 acres that ultimately would be transferred into the Kentucky Horse Park. This land changed ownership several times, until 1826, when Dr. William H. Richardson built the land into Kentucky's first farm, which he named Caneland, after the plentiful amount of cane growing near the plot's big spring. He created beautiful English gardens which included Kentucky's first greenhouse. Around 1840, Richardson became Kentucky's first landowner to establish a thoroughbred horse farm. Due to a cholera epidemic sometime in the late 1840's, the entire family was wiped out by the dreaded disease. In 1850, Eliphalet Muir married the niece of Daniel Boone, Anne Boone, both of whom reconstituted the horse farm, by raising Saddlebreds. Muir's death resulted in the transfer of ownership to S. J. Salyers, who continued developing Thoroughbreds. Salyers built a residence in 1866 that still exists as the present day offices of the horse park. By 1890, John D. Creighton aspired to ownership and constructed, in 1897, a training track, that is also still in use today. Eventually he suffered a foreclosure, when he lost the farm to creditors.

When two, Lexington, foreclosure bankers sold the land to a Colonel Milton Young, Young became owner of what is famously now Spindletop and Coldstream Farms. During Young's time, he originated a new practice of shipping several Standardbred yearlings for auction. When wealthy coal baron Captain Sam S. Brown bought not only the horses, but the entire farm, he renamed it Senorita Stud Farm, which memorialized one of his favorite mares. Brown was a key player in developing the Kentucky Association Racetrack in Lexington, which also led to his pivotal role in the Racetrack's evolution into the renowned Kenneland Racetrack. Further, he pioneered the development of water towers that pump water from wells which over the years have fed a plentiful supply of horses.

Brown eventually created such a good bloodline in his stock of horses that, in 1884, his horse named Buchanan won the Kentucky Derby. Brown's successor was Lamon V.

Harkness, who acquired the farm through an estate auction. Consequently, Harkness renamed the now famous farm Walnut Hill, which today has become one of the largest and best-known stables for Standardbred horses. By 1904, Harkness had enlarged the farm significantly from 450 acres and twelve mares in 1894, to 2,000 acres and one hundred mares in 1904. In 1897, he built the Big Barn, which is still standing today as a recognizable standard of the horse park. It is 476 feet long and has fifty-two stalls, as well as a sales area which is complete with an auction block. One of the largest horse barns ever built, it cost then a "whopping" $15,000! Ownership continued to spiral down the family chain, until 1947, when his grandson's wife, Mary Edwards, assumed ownership. She had married and become Mrs. Sherman Jenny. By the time she sold it in 1972 to the Commonwealth of Kentucky, it went for $2.7 million.

The Kentucky Horse Park opened to the public in 1978, when, as the world's only horse park, it was dedicated to man's relationship to the horse.

The park is one of the most popular attractions in Kentucky, if not for the entire world, especially for lovers of horse racing. The park has an impressive entrance highlighted by a memorial to *Man o' War*, as the renowned horse's burial site. A visitor's initiation to the park is achieved through a film about man's relationship with horses, which is narrated by William Shatner. The rest of the park comprises a self-guided tour and a horse-drawn trolley ride. After viewing the half hour Shatner film, visitors may then attend a live Breed Barn introduction to the several noted horses presently stabled in the Barn. Next comes the golden opportunity to meet the horses and their riders. The Hall of Champions offers a half hour film hailing many past champion horses. A fifty million-year history of the horse unfolds in an impressive, circular ramp which involves displays, artifacts, trophies, paintings, and carriages, in the International Museum of the Horse. Another close up opportunity allows visitors to visit the Big Barn which houses the work horses that pull the trolley.

Horseback riding and pony rides are also available. Allow two hours minimally for your visit.

The Ark

Another world-class, nearby, Kentucky attraction awaits. Take I-75N towards Cincinnati another 32 miles to Exit 120 at Williamstown, KY—The "Ark Encounter!" The drive is an easier one without the mountains, but also is slower and more congested, just fifty miles south of Cincinnati, OH.

Whatever your religion, the Ark Encounter features a full-sized replica of Noah's Ark, the only one in the World!

This reproduction comprises an almost unbelievably, gigantic confirmation of God's specifically ordered dimensions which He presented to Noah, and those that can be corroborated in every Christian Bible. Those dimensions translate from Bible language to present-day descriptions of 510 feet long, eighty-five feet wide, and fifty-one feet high. For sports and especially football *aficionados*, just imagine a building approaching two football fields long, over one fourth of a field wide, but then over four stories high; this modern engineering marvel astounds visitor's young and old! Most visits are crowded with tourists from all over the world.

THE ARK

The Bible's scriptural recitation, for the Ark in the St. Joseph's version of the Bible, begins in its first book entitled "Genesis," Chapter 6, verse 5: ." . . when the Lord saw how great was man's wickedness on earth . . . He regretted that He had made man." Verse 8 furthers God's opinion of his enamored choice of Noah with the words: "But Noah found favor with the Lord." Verse 14 directs Noah with the personally responsible directives: "Make yourself an Ark. . . ." Verse 18 offers God's explanation and plans as: "But with you I will establish my covenant; you and your sons, your wife, and your sons' wives, shall all go into the ark. . . ." Chapter 7, verse 12 contains God's "weather forecast" for Noah and his family as: "For forty days and forty nights heavy rain will be poured on the earth."

Chapter 9, verse 11 explains the religiosity involved: "I will establish my covenant with you, that never again shall all body creatures be destroyed by the waters of a flood. . . ." and verse 13 then finalized the heavenly symbol of this event as: "I set my bow in the clouds to serve as a sign of the covenant between me and the earth." This consists of God's confirmation of how "rainbows" would be forever attached to the earth's skies! These powerful biblical words describe the very reason for Noah's Ark.

The (Williamstown) Ark is the largest timber frame structure in the world, built from standing dead timber, in part by skilled Amish craftsmen. The Ark is an architectural and engineering marvel, containing a ground level plus three decks of world class exhibits. The four levels are accessible by inter-connecting ramps, as stairways were smartly avoided. Two or more areas have seating for viewing the short educational and quasi-religious, tutorial films. The ground level contains both the entry and the exit, on opposite ends of the structure, plus the Gift Shop.

Deck 1 has exhibits of models of small animals and their cages, a film tutorial with bench seating for "Introduction to Animal Kinds," an area exhibiting "Noah Gives Thanks," typical models of Ark Storage places, an exhibit on Bat Kinds, a Donor Wall honoring those philanthropic donors. In addition, this deck has ramps up, down, and between the deck above and ground floor below this level.

Deck 2 contains a second Gift Shop, the Ark Door, a display on "Who Was Noah," a reproduction of Noah's Study and Library, model examples of animal care areas, a compilation of animal kinds, a mural regarding Kid's Spooky Animal Encounters, the Noah Interview Theater, a Pre-flood world exhibit, a large display on Animal Encounters, and ramps up and down, both to and from decks 1 and 3.

Deck 3 has an exhibit regarding "Doors of the Bible," a display on "Why the Bible Is True," a large display on "Searching For Truth," a display on "Voyage of a Book," a Flood Legends exhibit, the Ancient Man exhibit, the Babel exhibit, the Ice Age exhibit, a Flood Geology exhibit, the "As in The Days of Noah Theater," models of Noah's Living Quarters, and similar ramps. Obviously, there's much to see, read, and absorb.

The Ark has many other exhibits on all three floors, and certainly is a great learning vehicle. Some of the educational and interesting subjects displayed include: how the Ark was constructed, with spectacular photographs; fascinating statistics, and much more. "How does it compare to the biblical description" is another question addressed. You'll learn how Noah most likely cared for the animals, and "How it was planned by Noah to fit his family of four couples in the same boat as the hundreds of animals." Another well-described subject is: "What do legends around the world believe about the great flood Noah had to survive?" Once you are in the "building," you can proceed at your own pace, view what you wish, take as much time as you desire, and enjoy the atmosphere within this massive structure.

Also located on the property outside the Ark are several separate fun stops for visitors. In the Ararat Ridge Zoo, camel rides and a petting zoo are available.

Emzara's Buffet has a scenic view of the bow of the Ark, while enjoying a buffet breakfast, lunch, or dinner. The Village market has both food eateries and a shopping area and is noted for their unique souvenirs.

The Screaming Eagle Zip Lines and Aerial Adventure are a challenge to willing visitors. The Answers Center has guest speakers or a short film on many varied but pertinent subjects in this new auditorium.

This attraction is one that should be included on not only every Christian's "bucket list," but also every person. Plenty of hotels are nearby. Allow three or four hours for maximum time to enjoy and observe all that is included in the Ark.

After a full day traveling, driving, and walking while touring two top attractions, and if you are on a trip to visit as much as possible in a limited amount of time, then making Ashland, KY, an overnight stop becomes a very good choice.

Two Key Travel Options

The trip to Ashland, KY, has two options. One is a little more time-consuming, extends through the heart of Appalachia, passes rural farms, has plenty of scenic views, traverses hilly terrain, and passes through several charming towns and villages. This more touristy option takes three hours and is approximately 104 miles, including only fourteen miles on I-64E. Directions include: from Williamstown, take St 22E three miles to Falmouth; continue on 22E to Brooksville twenty-five miles; change to Rt 9 SE six miles to Maysville; continue on Rt 9 southeast thirteen miles to Tollesboro; then continue again on St 9 another seventeen miles to Vanceburg; stay on St 9 SE an additional twenty-four miles to Grayson, which is on I-64. So use I-64E only fourteen miles to the Ashland exit; as hotels like the Hampton Inn are up just two miles on Cannonsburg Rd., on the right side back off the road.

The quicker, all interstate option, aggregates to 175 miles of I-75 and I-64, plus two miles off I-64 north to Ashland, KY. Obviously, this route is much longer, mileage-wise, less scenic, and somewhat backtracking from Williamstown, KY, to Ashland, KY. First, return/backtrack just a few short miles to I-75, then proceed south on I-75S to Lexington, KY, which is about fifty-five miles. From Lexington, KY travel east on I-64 approximately 115 miles through key towns like Winchester, KY, and Morehead, KY. A familiarization with mathematics could more easily explain that the shorter trip is the hypotenuse, and the longer trip comprises the two right angles of a measurable triangle form. So, make your choice!

Ashland, KY

Ashland has several good hotels, in addition to the Hampton Inn, a plentiful supply, with good choices of restaurants, and is a very charming town in itself.

The lovely town of Ashland, KY, is about ten miles further over Cannonsburg Road north to downtown, which is on the Ohio River. Across the river is the city of Ironton, in the "Buckeye State of Ohio."

A good restaurant for dinner—selectively if you like Italian food—might be the **Bellafonte Italian Restaurant** at 132 Carter Avenue.

Almost across Cannonsburg Road from the Hampton Inn—is a great breakfast restaurant that becomes a good option to start the day with a nice, hot, home-cooked meal at the **Bob Evans Restaurant.** Of course, Hampton Inns always offer their own free meal that just does't quite measure up to a fresh **Bob Evans** offering!

Ashland, KY, is on the southern bank of the Ohio River, with one bridge which extends into the State of Ohio. Ashland's population at

the 2010 census was 21,684, and is the smaller of the two primary cities, in the Huntington, WV/Ashland, KY, metropolitan area. Locally, the area is referred as the Tri-State Area, which has a combined population of 361,487, while the Kentucky portion alone is 110,641. Ashland is the regional center for Appalachia and has become a pivotal location in SE Kentucky for medical centers and economics.

Ashland's history dates back to the Poage family who relocated, from the Shenandoah Valley through the Cumberland Gap, in 1786. When the family erected a homestead on the Ohio River, they named it Poage's Landing, which others soon changed to Poage Settlement. That remained, until 1854, when the name was changed to Ashland, which was chosen as a memorial to Henry Clay's Lexington estate. Also, the name change reflected the city's growth and evolution into a burgeoning industrial town. The Ohio Valley's pig iron industry, along with the chartering of the Kentucky Iron, Coal, and Manufacturing Company by the Kentucky General Assembly in 1854, generated the city's early, industrial boom. The city was formally incorporated two years later, in 1856, by the State of Kentucky. Major industrial companies that evolved from this industrialization movement include Armco, Ashland Oil and Refining Company, the C&O Railroad, Allied Chemical & Dye Company's Semet Solvay, and Mansbach Steel. In retrospect, Ashland indeed made a good night's stopover, a good dinner, and Sunday Mass—all in preparation for the next leg into West Virginia and Virginia.

OHIO
Delaware
Dublin
Newark
Springfield
Columbus
Lancaster
71
77
Pittsburgh
Wheeling
Harrisburg
76
Morgantown
Cumberland
Hagerstown
MARYL
Parkersburg
Leesburg
Rockvil
Reston
Centreville
Wa
WEST VIRGINIA
Monongahela National Forest
Huntington
Charleston
Harrisonburg
Charlottesville
64
VIRGINIA
Richmond
Blacksburg
Roanoke
Petersburg

CHAPTER EIGHT

DESTINATION
BECKLEY, WV 133 MILES

The route to Beckley, WV, is quite direct, since it continues east on I-64E, just fourteen miles to Huntington, WV, and then fifty-two miles to the State Capital of Charleston, WV. The State of West Virginia is amongst the most picturesque in our nation. The roughly two-hour drive to Beckley, WV, is in itself, an amazingly beautiful, scenic example of the State's motto of "Wild and Wonderful." West Virginia's nickname is ""The Mountaineer State," which is evident every moment spent in this great state. At Charleston, WV, the interstate becomes much more scenic as it bends along and then over the Kawawha River, before it passes through a tunnel, and then up and down some very steep mountains almost all the way to Beckley. In Charleston, I-64 east and I-77 south conjoin and make one common highway, as it continues sixty-six more miles, until reaching Beckley, where it passes through the outskirts and just south of Beckley, WV.

Beckley, WV

Most of the Beckley hotels are on Harper Drive, either to one side or the other, at Exit 44 off of the combined interstates.

A usually excellent home-cooked, tasty breakfast awaits at the local **Cracker Barrel** restaurant, just west, up Harper Drive, on the right. This is a good option to the usual free, but ordinary Hampton Inn breakfast. Beckley's two excellent restaurants are both west off the same exit, with **Pasquale Mira's Italian Restaurant** on an off street, but similarly named, at 224 Harper Park Drive. **The Char,** Beckley's premier restaurant, is a little more hidden. After exiting west onto Harper Drive, the eatery is past the business district, a few short miles west on Harper Drive extension, then down into the valley on the left, at 100 Char Drive. The ride is worth the effort as the food, service, smooth background music, and atmosphere are superior.

Beckley, founded in 1838, was named in

memory of John James Beckley, the first clerk of the U.S. House of Representatives and the first Librarian of Congress. His son, Alfred Beckley, is the founder of Beckley, and was a U.S. Army lieutenant and brigadier general of the Virginia militia, in the Civil War. He was a native of the District of Columbia.

Almost humorously, the town at that time was only a "paper town," as it was physically non-existent. The town was then in the State of Virginia and finally became a "real" town in 1850, when the name was finalized from other names used of Beckleyville, Raleigh Courthouse, and sometimes Beckley.

Beckley is a favorite stopover for travelers, since three major U.S. highways all conjoin at a common intersection of prior-conjoined I-77 and I-64, plus US 19's southern termination, on the North side of Beckley. The city offers many choices of hotels, restaurants, and attractions for those who have time to enjoy Beckley. The most significant attractions are detailed below.

New River Gorge

North only thirty miles from Beckley, and just north of the smaller town of Fayetteville, WV (population 2,892), on super-highway US 19N, the New River Gorge National River

Park is either a half hour's drive from Beckley or a hop, skip, and a jump from Fayetteville. Dozens of qualified rafting firms attract thousands of would-be rafters who flock to the area yearly, to enjoy a thrilling, fun-filled day or two on one of America's greatest scenic combinations of key rivers and deep gorges. The New River gorge is over fifty miles long as it expands through one of the deepest gorges in America. The River is famous for its rapid, wild, and exciting channel, as rafters thrill at the many cataracts, some of which can measure sudden drops of over six feet. Rafters drive hundreds of miles, many on a regular basis, just to experience the euphoria and attack the challenge of a day spent testing the rugged, white water with one of the nation's longest continually dropping series of wild rapids. Available for all visitors, but especially so for photography loving visitors preferring only magnificent, beautiful views, the Canyon Rim National Park Visitors Center is just north over the New River Gorge Bridge on US 19N. The U.S. Government-operated Visitors Center provides outstanding overlooks of the gorge, the bridge, and the intriguing history related to the area. From the Government Visitors Center, there is a short nature walk for a panoramic, astounding view, from a wooden overview that looks over the river and the deep gorge. The walk is somewhat equivalent to three blocks, and is all paved and fairly level. Allow a half hour for this marvelous view.

If time permits, consider driving the Fayette Station Road, which winds down the steep gorge to the river for some fantastic, up-close, views of the bridge, the gorge, and the river. This scenic route was until 1977, the precursor route to the now world renowned bridge. There are a few riverside places to stop and walk closer to the edge of the roaring waters. Continuing up the river and against its sometimes brutal current, the old road eventually climbs back up on the opposite side, of the gorge, after crossing the only bridge in use at the level of the water's edge. The time spent and the drive is well worth the effort to see truly one of the wonders of the world, and more personally experience the "wild and wonderful" river!

NEW RIVER GORGE NATIONAL RIVER PARK

New River Gorge Bridge

A key part of the New River Gorge National River area is the magnificent New River Gorge Bridge. Located on US 19, just north of the town of Fayetteville, this world's wonder is the third highest bridge in the U.S. The bridge spans the New River 876 feet above the constant rush of its waters. The bridge is 3,030 feet long; its arch is 1,700 feet long, and for twenty-six years, after its opening in 1977, the bridge remained the world's longest, single-span, arched bridge. It is now the world's fourth longest! US 19 carries over

16,200 motor vehicles per day over this magnificent marvel of architecture.

Because of its height, the bridge attracts a steady stream of daredevils wanting to jump off the famous bridge. It is now the center piece of "Bridge Day," held every year when hundreds of people, with appropriate equipment, are permitted to climb up and jump off of the bridge. Also, it is the only time visitors or even locals are permitted to either walk or bike over the bridge.

NEW RIVER GORGE BRIDGE

When the bridge was completed, in late 1977, a long-standing, seriously infamous, travel problem was solved as it immediately cut off an additional forty plus minutes from the drive up or down US 19. From Beckley, and its connections to both I-64 and I-77, through the entire stretch of (new) US 19 north to I-79, just south of the town of Sutton, WV,

the entire sixty-eight mile route underwent a complete reconstruction as a very key linkage road. My wife and I recall with much annoyance, back in 1977, our attempt to drive the frequently detoured highway in and out of critical erection areas—the whole length of the sixty-eight mile reconstruction of this segment of US 19. This relatively short distance comprises a highly travelled, very key, U.S. connector highway. Interstate I-79 initiates in Charleston, WV and terminates in Erie, PA on Lake Erie, with Pittsburgh the chief city on its path. I-77 initiates at its most southern point in Columbia, SC and travels through major cities of both Charlotte, NC and Charleston, WV, while terminating its northern reach in Cleveland, OH. Interstate I-64 proceeds to its eastern termination at Norfolk, VA, and traverses to its western terminus in Lexington, KY. These major U.S. highways overwhelmingly point out the importance of upgrading the central West Virginia segment of US 19! This former patch of old US 19 contained the time-consuming and now scenic drive of the slow trudge down the gorge, along the visitor-congested river, and another slow flounder back up the steep walls of the gorge. In winters, this disguised "detour" was almost impossible to navigate, on some severe snow and ice days. In one instance at the new Bridge's opening, a hefty challenge magically became a work of structural art!

The sixty-eight-mile reconstructed highway north on US 19 is one of the most scenic in America, complete with some breath-taking views, and negatively, replete with many trucks. Realistically, both conjoining interstate highways, I-77 and I-64, also offer extraordinary scenery almost in every direction around Beckley. Fall foliage visitors to the entire geographical region comprise a huge share of local business, around the third week of October. During the winter, visitors come to West Virginia's snow and skiing resorts, also near Beckley. Certainly, Beckley's location, commerce, and attractions all combine to attract both travelers and vacationers, which all aggregate to make Beckley a frequent target destination year-round.

The Beckley Exhibition Coal Mine

Beckley has two outstanding, nationally listed and rated attractions: The Exhibition Coal Mine and the Tamarack West Virginia Artisan Center.

EXHIBITION COAL MINE

The Beckley Exhibition Coal Mine is an educational, historical, one-of-a-kind, and fun-filled "must-see" for travelers. The mine is located off I-77 / I-64 E, at Exit 44, also known as Harper Drive east. Harper Drive east continues past a highly commercial area of mostly motels and restaurants a few short miles to an offshoot street on the left named Ewart Avenue (513 Ewart Ave). Signs advertising the mine are frequent on the two conjoined interstate highways, and also along Harper Drive. The mine is part of the New River Park, and no doubt the most popular tour available as regards coal heritage destinations. A confirmation of the mine's status as a historical attraction is that the mine is listed on the National Register of Historic Sites. The huge administration building is also over the site of a large deep, underground coal mine on the outskirts of Beckley, WV. The structure contains a ticket office, souvenir store, and an excellent Coal Museum—

all available with the tour at one bargain price. The Coal Museum alone could suffice as a reason for the visit, with its very informative and educational opportunities. The Museum displays an extensive collection of mining artifacts and tools, geological specimens, photographs, and a homey assembly of features describing early life, in the surrounding coal towns of Southern West Virginia.

Its main attraction is the thirty-five-minute underground tour on operational authentic "man cars," which are guided by personable and experienced retired coal miners. The "man cars" hold approximately a dozen visitors, sitting opposite each other, sideways, in two vertical rows behind the tour guide. The cars operate on "working" mine tracks and move along at a steady pace, stopping only when the miner highlights or performs exhibits pertinent to the duties of coal miners of yesteryear. The former miner guide provided a very detailed, tutorial exhibition of how coal miners mined coal in years past, from low-seam, hand-loading, coal mining days of yesteryear, to the era of modern mechanization. Riding the authentic "man cars" underground and ducking when told to do so to eliminate the chance of hitting one's head, makes the experience more of a reality than with most such tours. Examples of coal mining duties and procedures are replicated at various sites of the mine, mimicking prior miner experiences. Frequently visitors are urged to walk a short stretch to witness the many techniques and tasks performed by the ex-miner. When not performing fascinating exhibits, the tour involves the miner's first-hand testimony of coal mining history, over a period of decades.

Disney World's Runaway Mine Train ride at its Orlando Magic Kingdom couldn't be a farther fetch from this authentic tour! This mine is the site of the former Phillips Family Mine that operated, from 1890 to 1910. Tours travel 1,500 feet below the surface of New River Park, which includes both the administration building and the mine.

Also part of the experience comprises a self-guided walking tour of the historical coal camp which surrounds the administration building and the mine. All camp structures have been carefully rebuilt and restored to illustrate an actual coal mining town. Included are the Coal Company House, Superintendent's Home, Pemberton Coal Camp Church, Miner's Shanty, and the Helen Coal Camp School. This reconstructed coal mining village comprises a true representation of early 20th century coal camp life.

The highly unique souvenir items offered in the store include local specialized food products, coal jewelry and figurines, children's underground helmets, clothing, historical books, and other interesting one-of-a-kind items. To conclude your visit, you can enjoy a delicious piece of home-made fudge! Allow two hours minimum for your visit. Visitors revel at the tour's authenticity, since it covers years of industry progression. And it comprises a fascinatingly enjoyable adventure.

The Tamarack Artisan Center

The Tamarack Artisan Center is located off conjoined I-77 and I-64 and, just north of Beckley. Also, it is attached to Beckley, just off Harper Drive. It is well advertaised along the interstates for travelers to the area. Tamarack has developed from originally a traditional rest stop to a full-fledged, artisan center. The successful pioneering, by former West Virginia Governor Gaston Caperton, enabled Tamarack to expand both as a fine arts center and a specialized food stop when their new modern facility opened in 1995. It has become a vibrant cottage industry for West Virginia jobs, marketing opportunities, artisan showcases and exhibitions, crafts people, food producers, and perhaps more importantly, a popular travelers' target for its hand-made artisan crafts and home-made West Virginia food treats. Its motto has all along been "The Best or West Virginia!"

TAMARACK WEST VIRGINIA ARTISAN CENTER

Beginning as just a thought for improving on simply a "rest stop," Tamarack's legacy is that of the very first showcase of handcrafts, fine art, and regional cuisine along any interstate in the nation. It exudes a friendly atmosphere, an attractive and unique both external and internal design, and is located off a busy set of parallel interstates, which are conjoined to the origination of US 19N. Tamarack feeds off of the fast-growing economic center of Beckley. It incorporates a retail store, working studios for resident artisans, a fine art gallery, a theater, the "A Taste of West Virginia" food court, and the Tamarack Conference Center, which hosts local, state-wide, and national company and organizational conferences.

This pioneering state-wide project began in 1989, after a careful study of economic potential. Earlier, it comprised local artisan products that then were offered individually at existing rest stops in the state. The study especially honed in on this prime location outside of Beckley. Once approved and adopted, the project delivered almost sudden and amazing success, as compared to other existing West Virginia travel stops.

Artisans were involved in the project by creating both structural elements to the building itself, as well as to step up its recruitment of state-wide artisans, for future jobs, benefits, and careers.

The state's most well-known resort and iconically famous national attraction just east, one hour on I-64—**The Greenbrier America's Resort**—agreed to assist with food service management; this ensured that the quality in the food offered at this first-of-a-kind site would be and still is as a gourmet eatery. At the groundbreaking on August 8, 1994, visitors sampled tastes from the **Greenbrier,** which included an old West Virginia favorite of fried green tomatoes. Ever since that inauguration of upscale food, that old favorite dish has since become a signature at Tamarack.

The conference center opened in 2003, which completed what was labelled in 1994 as "West Virginia's Bold Experiment." Today, this first of the nation's artisan centers, now includes over 2,800 artisans from all of West Virginia's fifty-five counties, revenues top $78 million, and purchases of goods and services have revived the state's coffers, with an additional $65 million tax base. Their parking lot seems always full! If you appreciate arts and crafts and prefer gourmet food over "fast food," then you should add Tamarack to your traveler's "bucket list."

Coal Heritage Trail

Beckley, WV is famously described as the regional center of the southern West Virginia smokeless coal industry. The bituminous coal that is locally mined in this region produces a higher grade of coal when burnt. Beckley is the northern anchor of the legendary 187-mile Coal Heritage Trail that adventurously curves, climbs mountains, and drops into deep valleys through 500 small coal mining towns. These mostly little, homesteader burgs comprise miners houses, railroads, company stores, and coal tipples along the way from Beckley to Bluefield, WV.

Recommended as an abbreviated, but perhaps more exemplary version of the Coal Heritage Trail, is a reduced 102 mile side-trip. Mustering a half day of excelling scenery through mountain woodlands, historic remnants of yesteryear, and two most interesting, celebrated coal towns, The Coal Heritage Trail has proven to have been a richly rewarding detour that vaguely and comparably parallels I-77. This old and delightful highway was the forerunner of I-77, as it stretches from Beckley, WV to Virginia. The Coal Heritage Trail proceeds southwest from Beckley on SR 16 only fifty-five miles to first Welch, WV.

Welch, WV

Welch is a unique "ground zero" for the captivating history of coal mining. With a population from 2010's latest census of 2,406, this town has certainly played a key role in the ups and downs of coal mining history.

Welch, WV has been the county seat of McDowell County since 1893, when it was incorporated. It was named after a captain in the Confederate Army, Isaiah A. Welch. The captain became a land surveyor who played a major role in drawing up a plan for the town, which is at the confluence of the Tug Fork River and Elk Horn Creek.

WELCH COUNTY WV HISTORIC COURTHOUSE

No trip is complete without stopping to see and experience the phenomenal history of the Welch, WV Historic Courthouse. Few, if any, counties can claim that the grounds

of the courthouse played a prominent role in the area's somewhat crazy history. Not since the late 1800's has any other courthouse played such a role in hanging its constituents for felonious crimes. The infamous Hanging Judge of Fort Smith, AK is the only other such scenario that comes to memory from this history buff.

An example of the strange, wild-west types of activity follows, right out of the history of the area. Taken from the article written by Bob Powell, the West Virginia Public Broadcasting's Radio Operations Director states the following, as I quote:

"On August 1, 1921, Matewan police chief Sid Hatfield and his friend Ed Chambers were gunned down by Baldwin-Felts detectives in front of the McDowell County Courthouse in Welch.

The trouble between Hatfield and the Baldwin-Felts had started more than a year earlier. In May of 1920, a shootout in the Mingo County town of Matewan had pitted Baldwin-Felts detectives against Hatfield and a crowd of angry miners.

A shoot-out left seven of the detectives, two miners, and the town's mayor dead in the streets of Matewan.

After the Matewan Massacre, as it's now known, Hatfield became a hero to the miners who were trying to unionize southern West Virginia. The Baldwin-Felts detectives decided to take revenge against Hatfield after he and 17 others were acquitted of all charges related to the massacre.

They seized their chance when Hatfield and Chambers were set to appear at the McDowell County Courthouse on charges unrelated to the earlier shootout. Hatfield's murder sparked an uprising that led weeks later to an armed march on Logan County and the Battle of Blair Mountain, the largest single conflict of the Mine Wars."—end quote!

Other obtained information declares that the Battle of Blair Mountain was the only battle in history where the US government bombed its own citizens by plane.

Just down the street from the courthouse, the last execution in McDowell County by the Circuit Court occurred when John Hardy was hanged for killing a man over 25 cents in a game of dice. Hardy has been memorialized in some of the earliest folk music, entitled "John Hardy." All of this murderous activity took place at a time in West Virginia history when mining came under fire due to a change in methods, caused mostly by the dawning of mechanization in the local mines.

The present-day town strangely became a county seat in 1892, even before it offcially had become an incorporated city. At the time the county seat was Perryville (now English, WV). When the results of the election for determining which town deserved the title of county seat were contested, in order to avoid any violence, two citizens took it upon themselves to secretly move the election records overnight to Welch. When in March of 1921, the city council in Welch met to discuss impeaching the Mayor, the Mayor showed up at that meeting and disrupted the impeachment process. The city council countered by asking the local sheriff to investigate the actions of the Mayor.

However, later that same day the Mayor shot the deputy sheriff who had been chosen as the investigating officer. Although the Mayor was arrested and charged with murder, he was freed when he got away by falsely claiming that the investigator's testimony had been perjured. In September of 1921, the corrupt, murdering Mayor fled the area, never to be seen again, Scott-free! To continue this sad saga, in August of 1921 detectives with a private agency assassinated both the police chief and another person at the county courthouse.

Over the first half of the 20th century, Welch became a prosperous major city of 100,000 citizens. This resulted from the opening of railroads and coal mines throughout the area. Welch was a hub of retail businesses, and boasted of having three hospitals. However this changed after World War II, when oil began its measured substitution for coal for households and other domestic fuel needs. Further changing the economic landscape of Welch was the gradual changeover to mechanization of coal mines, which drastically reduced the number of coal miners employed in local coal mines. Around 1950, McDowell County's population peaked, then began a steady decline over the following decades. History would indicate that perhaps Welch's last hurrah happened around 1960, when the declining city claimed its moniker of "The Heart of the Nation's Coal Bin." At that particular time, that claim was done with justification, since McDowell County still ranked number one in the U. S. in total coal production.

When presidential candidate John F. Kennedy's motorcade passed through Welch in 1960, the city was struggling with a fast growing poverty rate throughout all of McDowell County. It was later revealed that Kennedy and his running mate, Lyndon Johnson, used Kennedy's opinions of a weak economic situation in Appalachia for a bundle of financial aid that they later brought to the area. During a speech in not-too- distant Canton, Ohio on September 27, 1960, Kennedy stated: "McDowell County mines more coal than it ever has in its history, probably more coal than any county in the United States. The reason is that machines are doing the jobs of men, and we have not been able to find jobs for those men."

Consequently, the Chloe and Alderson Muncy family of Paynesville, WV, residents of McDowell County, became the first recipients of modern era food stamps. This occurred when in May of 1961, Kennedy's Secretary of Agriculture presented the Muncy family $95 worth of federal food stamps. This first time incident with food stamps became the precursor of the rapid expansion of federal assistance legislated as part of the Democratic theme of the "War On Poverty."

The modern city's pet project is very unique in both embellishing the local area with color, and ordering an opportunity for locals to make a few bucks on the side. The City of Welch Lavender Project may help restore the area's former profitable interest in agriculture, as some locals feel that coal has driven out other forms of income for the area. Promoting a new creatively-introduced Lavender project, may just be the commercial growth button the area needs to replace some of the economic value that disappeared in recent years. Mechanization is the chief culprit of why nearby coal mines either declined drastically, closed all-together, or most certainly coal jobs decreased significantly.

Lavender is the highest profit per acre item that can be grown legally. Although producing sufficient acreage of lavender required for a usual harvest could be the disdaining issue—especially for citizens of a small city, the product could possibly become exceptionally separated from mass production. Despite a lack of large acreages of property to be used as a farm, local residents in Welch usually own homes with very large yards. As a result, the marketing plan recommends that these citizens use their properties to, each, plant ten lavender bushes. In this manner, the city becomes more attractive when the bushes are in bloom, and the owners that participate form a co-operative group that shares in the combined harvest, which is made possible by commingling on the production sufficiently to participate in a normal harvest. Both homeowners and the city benefit from this new engagement with economic well-being.

Throughout the score of years consisting of the 60's and 70's, McDowell County continued as a key supplier of coal energy for the steel and electric power industries. However, McDowell County suffered economically in lock step with the decline in steel production. Concomitantly, as major steel manufacturers' coal mines began closing in the area, jobs were also lost. Personal incomes declined by two-thirds! When the economic depression escalated into real estate losses, miners were forced to relocate far away, or minimally to other places within the Country.

In 2006 further adverse county-wide imprecations were amplified when Welch's police chief was charged with a claim of wrongful death. This resulted from the chief's interference of rescuers attempting to apply CPR to a gay man who was suffering cardiac arrest. This lawsuit was promptly, secretly, and quietly settled without any additional mention.

Good news finally came to Welch when new state and federal prisons were build in the rural County. This created some economic recovery with new jobs and other related services tantamount to a prison. Tourism has been added to the local economy in recent years, when the city won federal funds to restore its historic downtown area. In the past, Welch has hosted high level celebrities to their annual Veteran's Day Parade, including Presidents Truman and Johnson.

Over the years, Welch has boasted of some positive nationally-acclaimed, first-time achievements. These have rekindled, first the preponderance of community activities, which years later became the warmest memories of locals. These have included the first public playground for children, the first memorial to fallen service men and women, the first black woman (state) legislator, and the first municipally concomitantly-owned and operated public garage.

The Sterling Drive-in Restaurant

The top, iconic restaurant in Welch is the Sterling Drive-in, located at 788 Stewart Street, phone number 304-436-3271. Locals flock to this genuine throw-back drive-in restaurant with its home-cooked selection of scrumptious food, headlined with a tasty, prime burger—grilled, seasoned, and served to perfection. Customers have a choice of eating outside with a car-hop, or inside in their simplistic, attractive dining room. Menu choices cover the entire day from AM egg varieties, to salads or burgers for lunch, and either sandwiches or

STERLING DRIVE-IN

gourmet meals at dinner—all at some of the most economic prices found anywhere. In addition to its popularized burger reputation, other favorites include: West Virginia Style Hot Dogs (mustard, chili, onion and slaw); tender, juicy steaks; chicken, greek, and pasta choices. According to locals, the most popular identifiable selections include: the Sterling Signature Sub (secret sub spread, cranberry sauce, bacon, and toppings), the Sterling Special (ham and cheese sub), the Fat Boy double cheeseburger, and the bountiful salads. The milkshakes are ohhhh so legendary and yummy! People who frequent the restaurant have eaten at the Sterling for generations, and those who move away, always return when making visits to Welch.

Truly there has been centuries full of meaningful history emanating from Welch and its surrounding McDowell County. Obviously most of it is positive, but some has been downright demeaning. Obviously, what is chiefly noteworthy is that the Welch and McDowell County region has earned a nationally-known economical reputation for their key role in West Virginia's chief coal industry.

From Welch, follow US52 southeast forty-seven miles to its termination in charmingly old fashioned Bluefield. Bluefield, WV also serves as the largest city on the abbreviated drive from Beckley, down through the gorgeous Appalachian Mountain chain, and ultimately back to I-77 South, and thus terminating West Virginia's Coal Heritage Trail tour.

With a present, significantly diminished population from yesteryears of only 10,447, Bluefield is none-the-less regarded as the geographical and economic center of the two-state combined micropolitan area. That region is shared with the State of Virginia, which has a combined sizable population of 107,342!

Bluefield, WV

The Bluefield area had its beginning in the late 1700's when two families migrating from Europe homesteaded in the area. The population grew exponentially as the original family recruited many more immigrants from their European homelands. This influx of primarily white settlers built a small village consisting of a mill, a church, a one-room schoolhouse, and surrounded their new settlement with a protective fort.

Unfortunately, unbeknownst to these new settlers, they had built their new establishment in a location infringing on a Shawnee Indian tribe. Nearby, the Shawnee had built a sizable village on the banks of the Bluestone River, which made life more than merely uncomfortable for both the pioneers and the Shawnee!

Most locals explain one version of how the city earned its name, which has emanated down through the years since that first pioneering settlement. That rendition instigated from the abundance of chicory flowers which grow throughout the area. When the chicory flowers are in full bloom, there is a purplish blue hue that radiates from the surrounding countryside during the summer. However, another version of the naming of the city seems more identifiable, as most feel it probably came from the development of the coal fields in that area of the Bluestone River.

Early roots of the city's development date from 1882, when pioneering businessmen built the Norfolk & Western Railroad through the hills and mountains of the area. This very key project ballooned southern West Virginia's already burgeoning economic development of its coal industry. Prospectors soon discovered that beneath the Bluefield area lay the World's largest and richest deposit of bituminous coal! The first locally highly promising seam of the "black gold" was discovered in a settler's back yard. The head of the Norfolk & Western Railroad described this event as the "most spectacular find on the continent and indeed perhaps of the entire planet."

Surprisingly, this very seam had been mentioned many years earlier by Thomas Jefferson's "notes on the State of Virginia," since West Virginia was still part of Virginia for many decades. Finally, the seam became a mine in 1890. The development of new coal mines near a grouping of four separate cities evolved into the widely known identification as the Pocahontas Coal Fields. This regional mining expansion, coupled by a surging railroad movement, combined to instigate a key role in the Country's development and participation in the Industrial Revolution. The entire national, as well as especially local economy enjoyed a period of booming growth. That economic insurgence was transpired by the relocation of thousands of both migrants from Europe and enslaved/migrant African-Americans from the Deep South. In the late 1800's the Norfolk & Western Company chose Bluefield as its headquarters and repair center, which greatly expanded the city's growth. In just one year from 1887 to 1888 Bluefield grew by a whopping 317%! During both World Wars coal from the southern West Virginia region surrounding Bluefield supplied the navies from both the United States and United Kingdom.

The thriving city of Bluefield strained to

handle such an unprecedented population growth. The city's infrastructure became incapacitated to handle the new arrivals. Housing quickly became unprepared to handle the "overnight" growth. Workers were forced to exist in crowded, outdated quarters, often without their families. The Railroad controlled the economy, as Bluefield vacillated from growth to decay and back again repetitiously. When coal tonnage shipments were booming, Bluefield earned the moniker of "Little New York." The sprawling metropolis had a nightlife, and a character identification with other large U.S. cities that included "a little bit Chicago," "a little bit New York," and a "mostly Pittsburgh." The closest connection to "The Smokey City" was due to Pittsburgh's similarly rough-nosed psyche, and comparable economies of both coal and steel embedded into its soul.

The nearby, formerly small village of Bramwell, WV, just incorporated in 1888, was characterized as "Millionaires Town," with all the new money that poured into the local economy, banking, and structure. It was said at that time that more millionaires per capita lived in the Bluefield area than any other place in the Country! Also, Bluefield's roads became over-crowded when the city's administrators confirmed that Bluefield contained more autos per capita than any other U.S. city. Belatedly, Bluefield became incorporated in 1889.

The trend towards a strong, well-educated ethnic community aspired in 1895, to the foundation of the Bluefield Colored Institute, which has evolved today into Bluefield State College.

Bluefield thrived as a metropolis and leading shipper of coal tonnage until the Great Depression in 1929. On that dark day in history, Bluefield's government became bankrupt, its city structures were completely razed by a string of all-encompassing fires through the downtown area, and its previously bellwether shipments of coal disintegrated almost overnight. Unfortunately this economic disaster lasted for over a decade until the outbreak of World War II. Bluefield had become so strategically important as to make Adolph Hitler's list of targeted air raids, which fortunately never occurred. However the city held regular air raid drills at the time, which called attention to their explained apprehension.

Bluefield suffered one final catastrophe when the Interstate Highway System finished

construction of the close-by East River Mountain tunnel for I-77 on December 20, 1974. This modern-day high speed highway eliminated the prior requirement of long-distance north-south drivers necessarily having to use West Virginia's backroads up and down steep mountains as their only mode of transportation through the State.

Since the tunnel bypassed the mountains surrounding Bluefield, the city lost substantial traffic, jobs, and ultimately population, in one fell sweep! The latest economic calamity to hit Bluefield was the closing of the local Amtrak station in the 1980's.

Unfortunately there are no outstanding touristy attractions readily available at the time of writing this travel book. The most popular activity is riding ATV's up and down the many miles of the Hatfield & McCoy mountain trails, just south of the area. Although there seems to be a plentiful amount of overnight stay places, unless travelers bring their own ATV's, local ATV rentals are sold our weeks in advance of spontaneous trips by most travelers.

Truly, the historical sequencing for West Virginia's esteemed coal industry, the many reminders of that boom era, and the unequaled mountain scenery all combine for a fascinating opportunity to experience still one of history's and nature's best offerings in America. Just by engaging half a day's drive down the Coal Heritage Trail, travelers can experience a most worthy day's sojourn.

The portion of I-77 south (or north) from Beckley to Princeton, WV, which almost conjoins with Bluefield, is forty-five miles of majestic scenic highway.

CHAPTER NINE

DESTINATION
LEXINGTON, VA 133 MILES

Greenbrier Hotel

The nationally recognized tourist destination of White Sulphur Springs, WV, is the iconic Greenbrier Hotel, which carries the famous motto as "America's Resort." From Beckley, travel east forty-three miles on I-64 to Exit 175, then follow signs to White Sulphur Springs—just a few miles right on US 60E to the world-famous hotel; it's location is 101 Main Street West. The parking lot is eternally so crowded that daytime visitors are scurried into the train station parking lot, about the equivalence of three to four block's walk back to the hotel. The hotel offers free gold cart rides, or visitors may choose walking instead. These are the only two options to reach the hotel. Once a first-time visitor comes into eye contact with the hotel, its magnanimity seems overwhelming. The Greenbrier is perhaps the most stately and statuesque hotel in the country. Just walking the heavily carpeted floors and relishing the well-designed and decorated interior easily defines the long history of the structure. However, history soon evolves economically into "today," when a first-time visitor witnesses the constant flurry of drop-offs, arrivals, and departures from guests to this national treasure. Part of the entrance embellishment consists of the outside, detached guest houses that line the driveway onto the property. The guest houses are also stately, well-conditioned, and add to the historical pattern of the immediate area.

In addition to its architectural and historical fame, The Greenbrier has hosted such signature sports events as the Ryder Cup and PGA professional golf tournaments. Also, it annually hosts professional football's Houston Texans' summer training camp.

Bunker Tour

In the basement of the Greenbrier Hotel resided perhaps the U.S. Government's best and longest kept secret, for over thirty years from 1961 to 1992! Not until May 31,1992, did anyone outside of a small staff of sworn, secretive U.S. Government key employees know about the now infamous "Project Greek Island," which we presently identify as the Eisenhower era's underground bunker. The fascinating "bunker tour" experience—almost thirty years after its exposure by a Washington Post reporter—still remains publicly unknown yet today. Although today, Americans recognize on the "bunker tour" that it now has a historical remembrance as a former strategic fortress of magnanimous and spacious proportions. The facility contains 112,544 square feet of well-designed, once highly and actively readied, and an extraordinarily secured fortress. One-hour tours are offered daily with reservations, since only twenty-five persons may take the tours with very informed, personable, and experienced guides.

Much walking is required but to see all of its rooms, power stations, security equipment, and housing areas, an encompassing visit necessitates hiking up and down several sets of steep steps. The tour initiates in the back lobby of the hotel, near the elevators to the guest rooms.

The purpose for such a sizable bunker was thought out in the era of the atomic bombs and heightened Cold War, with then enemy Russia. It was planned out that all members of Congress could escape Washington, D. C., by bus safely, in one hour and reach a secured place, before the plausible time-period arrival of an enemy bomber airplane reaching the Capitol. The securitization includes four entrances, three to The Greenbrier's grounds and one to the main, fortressed building. Its entrance consists of a 25-ton blast door that opens only with fifty pounds of pressure. There

are decontamination chambers consisting of highly chemical cleansing "showers," eighteen dormitories which are designed to house over 1,000 Congressmen (including women), a power plant with purification equipment, and three 25,000 gallon water storage tanks. The communications area included television production and audio recording booths. A health clinic was maintained with twelve hospital beds, medical and dental offices, and an operating room. There was a laboratory, pharmacy, intensive care unit, cafeteria, and official meeting rooms for each of the two congressional chambers: The House and The Senate. It was maintained twenty-four hours every day and user-ready anytime for immediate occupancy all during the thirty years plus that it remained secretive. Both houses of Congress were on separate levels (floors) under, and hidden from, the hotel proper.

In its later years, concerns arose that a combination of more modern airplanes, missiles, and more powerful bombs almost dismissed the safety and effectiveness required to protect the Congress. It then was realized that Congressmen no longer would be able to reach the bunker safely.

As a result of the thirty years that it

remained a readied, protective bunker, the time had come to end this project. However, the secrecy was kept, until May 31,1992, when a Post reporter wrote an exposing article entitled "The Last Resort." Immediately, the government declassified and closed the bunker. This allowed the owners of the property, The Greenbrier Hotel, to retake control and to turn this historical long kept secret into a tour that over the years has become the key attraction, as it remains today. The tour is a thought-provoking and memorable revisit of the long Cold War and how the U.S. Government planned to care for its critically important legislative wing.

White Sulphur Springs, WV

White Sulphur Springs is a small, charming city, with an interesting main street of shops and restaurants. The population in 2018 was estimated at 2,398. The city's emblem consists of five dandelion flowers, so its most celebrated local event every spring is the Dandelion Festival. The city was known as the southern "Queen of the Watering Places," during the early 1800s. Its springs became a successful resort for Virginia's wealthy Low Country residents, as a summer cooling off retreat. It eventually attracted summer visitors from all over the South, ultimately gaining fame as a socially exclusive retreat for the wealthy. If there ever could be such a place in America voted as the idyllic definition of "Main Street America," then White Sulphur Springs, WV would win that contest every day!

The city supports it's "drawing card" resort, known worldwide as The Greenbrier, which remains one of the most luxurious and exclusive resorts in America.

An excellent luncheon stop is 50 East Main, a combination restaurant/bar, with very tasty hamburgers, and cheeseburgers among other sandwiches. The **luncheon emporium** is further east of The Greenbrier, on Main Street, about a mile of so on the left.

White Sulphur Springs National Fish Hatchery

The White Sulphur Springs National Fish Hatchery was established in 1900, and is located on the opposite side of the town from the hotel, at the far eastern end of Main Street. The hatchery developed from the early era Midland Trail that crossed the heart of the Allegheny Highlands of Southeast West Virginia. Over the years, the hatchery has supplied the area's rivers and lakes with plentiful fish stocked for the pleasure and sport of surrounding citizens. In 1976, the hatchery became enjoined to the National Broodstock Program. Since then, it has shipped millions of disease-free rainbow trout eggs to other national, state, and tribal hatcheries across the nation.

A new program was incepted in 1995 regarding freshwater mussel conservation. The sterling results have created a shelter for mussels threatened by pollution, and raised baby mussels to improve and increase wild populations.

> **"The Mission of the White Sulphur Springs National Fish Hatchery is working with the community and the various partnership relationships it has developed over the years. Its definition is to continue as good stewards of both the environment and historical significance by providing recreational fishing opportunities and recovering mussels and other wildlife and their habitats. Finally, its official duties include promoting awareness and appreciation of the peoples cultural and natural resources that benefit all the Nation's citizens."**

Lexington, VA

Lexington, VA, is seventy miles farther east on I-64E from White Sulphur Springs. The drive into Virginia is beautiful, scenic, and impressively mountainous, as we all know their State motto of "Virginia Is for Lovers!"

The city is fifty-seven miles inside of Virginia from

West Virginia, at the intersection of I-64 and I-81. At the last census in 2010, the population was 7,042.

Lexington is the home of the Virginia Military Institute (VMI) and of Washington and Lee University (W&L). In 1778, it was named the first like-named city of what would eventually become the same-name also for many other U.S. cities, after Lexington, MA, an historical city steeped in the history of The Revolutionary War; The first shot of that War was fired in Lexington, MA.

Lexington, VA, is perhaps the best combination of a good overnight stay for our next-day's much anticipated, daylong trip to Cass, WV, for the train trip up Bald Knob Mountain, and a much more efficient stepping off location, for the upcoming, long driving day, two days later, as our first leg heading home to SW Florida. An interesting development occurred when we went the ten miles into downtown Lexington, for dinner. The downtown of Lexington sits on hilly terrain and was designed with a tight grid of one-way streets lined with shops, restaurants, and bars. When we stopped in front of a half dozen restaurants at the nearest parking place, surprisingly most establishment eateries claimed they were busy with longer than desired wait times.

Two outwardly (and honestly) announced that their

restaurant was open exclusively for locals only! WOW! In all of our years of traveling this nation, we had never received such a cold and rejective welcome to a new city.

However, happily for us, we quickly recalled, as we have done several times on the road, that sometimes neighborhood bars, too, have decent food.

So, we discovered **"The Palms,"** which fortunately served a very delicious, Monday night "on special" meal of fish and home-made chips. We were so enamored of **"The Palms,"** for its friendliness, hustling wait persons, and, quite honestly, surprisingly very tasteful meal. So, the next night, we simply repeated the experience and loved the dinner once more. If you go to Lexington, we highly recommend **"The Palms"** for dinner anytime.

Just for the record, Lewisburg, WV, is also an alternative stopover for Cass, WV, if you desire a quick, westward departure the day after the train ride, obviously the opposite direction of our routed direction towards home. Also, for the record, Cass itself has proven to be a great night's stay, with their very economically friendly, clean, quiet, cabins, rental homes and access to the train, if you have the time to allow for that great option! Renting a former miner's whole house—and for a price equal to only one motel room—would have again for us been a preferred option, if we hadn't routed our trip home, in a time-sensitive manner.

CHAPTER TEN

DESTINATION LEXINGTON, VA
(VIA CASS, WV) 79 MILES
(ROUND TRIP TOTAL 158 MILES)
(SECOND NIGHT IN LEXINGTON)

The two hour drive to Cass, WV, is very scenic, mountainous, and filled with sharp curves, through the heart of the majestic Appalachian Mountains. Most of the trip is in West Virginia—thus supporting its nickname of "The Mountaineer State!" From Lexington take the road directly in front of the Hampton Inn, VA ST RD 39 west fifty-five miles into WV, to the little burg of Minnehana, WV. Then switch to WV ST RD 92 north 10 miles to Frost, WV. Continue on the same road another seven miles to Dunmore, WV. Then take WV ST RD 28 4 more miles north to its junction with WV ST RD 66 west.

Make a left onto WV ST RD 66 west three miles to our destination, the very special, but small town of Cass, WV. Total miles driven should be seventy-nine from Lexington.

The train's huge, dirt/gravel parking lot is immediately on the right, just before the tracks. The ticket office, the famous Last Run Restaurant, grocery/general/souvenir store, and rest rooms are all in the huge, freshly-painted, and recently refurbished building that overlooks the train and tracks. Walking a somewhat steep hill, plus climbing the many steps into the building may be a difficult task for some visitors. Instead, walk up the paved road to the top of the hill in front of the yellow headquarters building. Rather than climb the many steps to the front of that building, choose to walk in front of the building until the number of steps decline, near the back of the building. All doors that enter the building lead to interconnected rooms, consisting of all the above listed related stops that support the train. If perhaps you are staying overnight or for a few days in one of the refurbished, two story, clean as a whistle, old, mining company houses, the village and residences are to the left of the street that continues up the hill, with the huge building on the right. Rental homes are to the left, just a short one or two block walk.

We spent one night there and enjoyed the quiet, and convenience to the train. Also we had a good dinner and breakfast at the historic **Last Run Restaurant**.

Many visitors, especially with large families and groupings, rent a house, as all houses include a usable kitchen, so if desired, overnighters can cook for themselves, buying their food, *et. al.* at the store in the big, yellow building.

In the historic town of Cass, its reconstructed and refurbished structures remain relatively unchanged, since its founding in 1901 by particularly the West Virginia Pulp and Paper Company. However, its present population of eighty-two tells the story that Cass is purely a tourist-based attraction. However, Cass' dramatic history rules the present, especially during the town's rebirth each spring, as Cass seasonally opens its dynamic railroading ventures.

Cass was built by the company town to house the logging workers and their families. Considering its role in the bygone days of old, the mountain town's heydays date to the beginning of the 20th century, when it was a large, lumbering community stuck way up in the mountains. It seems logical to recognize why hauling cut lumber with the trains from far up into the nearby mountains down to the Cass lumber mills was a key industry in those days.

Cass, WV, is a town now famous for the Cass Scenic Railroad, perhaps one of the nation's most popular and most accessible attractions, by huge population areas of the U.S. Many highly populated cities of America are within a one day's drive of this marvel! The diminishing trend of railroad train trips in the U.S. also makes Cass, WV, a favored destination for the type of attraction that Cass still offers today. Cass has become a magnet for the State of West Virginia, with the Cass Scenic Railroad State Park no doubt the state's key crowd pleaser. Spending time in Cass makes understanting why "Wild & Wonderful" have become the state's motto. It becomes a momentary reaction, especially in this gorgeous region of West Virginia, to initiate singing aloud John Denver's, and now West Virginia's State Song, "Country Roads."

Because of the staunch "railroader" attraction to Cass, the referral in the "Introduction" section of this book requested readers to seek out the internet web site for "Cass Scenic Railroad Appalachian Fall Foliage" and listen to the engaging, scintillating steam whistle!

Cass Scenic Railroad

The world's largest fleet of geared Shay locomotives resides in Cass. Five Shays, one Heisler, and one Climax combine to form the largest grouping active today of primarily Shay locomotives. The oldest operable Shay in existence is the C-80 Shay #5, that has been toiling up Cheat Mountain on the way to Bald Knob, since around the year 1900!

CASS SCENIC RAILROAD

Now it's time to get excited, since you are about to take a trip back to an era when steam-driven locomotives were an essential part of everyday life. As the engines hook up the train cars, visitors enjoy their first introduction to the blast of the steam whistle which resonates down the entire valley. Wooo, wooo, wooo, I can still hear that scintillating sound through my imagination! That memorable moment can become a seldom heard song that briefly triggers a case of euphoria for most train buffs! June 2019 was our third visit and we can attest that the euphoria feeling that third time was still there!

THE SEVEN PHASES OF THE

FIRST: The welcome as the train departs Cass—those first scintillating blows of the whistle that signify in traditional railroad "language" the time for departure!

SECOND: The switch-back where the engine becomes the booster!

THIRD: Whitaker Station!

FOURTH: The point where the goal of Bald Knob is noticed—far away!

FIFTH: Second watering stop, where passengers can spend time out of the train observing the trains watering and switching, plus witness the steep declines over the side of the mountain!

SIXTH: Welcome to Bald Knob, and especially the wooden overlook deep into the valley far below!

SEVENTH: Good-bye, again in train language, with the final blows of the whistle!

CASS SCENIC RAILROAD

One of the lesser, but still also impressive experiences, is at the switch back, just before approaching Whitaker Station, on the way up the mountain. The engine pulls the train up the first mountain, and then just before the second steep incline before Whitaker Station, uses the second parallel track to reposition the engine from the front of the train to the back of the train in order to better push the train up the upcoming most difficult stretch of the trip. The switchback becomes a fascinating opportunity to marvel, as the trip begins to arouse anticipation for more newfangled, highly adventurous experiences, that seem just around the corner.

One specific recollection comes from a point rather early on the uphill climb, while the train climbs the mountain, when the conductor points out the location of Bald Knob, the very ultimate target for the trip. At the moment that the conductor makes his directive, Bald Knob appears for a short time still several miles away, and at quite a distance several mountains away and much higher than the train's present position. That scene becomes one of the most impressive memories of the whole trip. The engine's tugging strain of hauling tons of weight while climbing steep angles seemed difficult to continue at that point. Since one could see far ahead what those engines had yet to accomplish, in retrospect, it would comprise a tremendous feat especially for train engines that have aged over 120 years! What a marvel such an experience must have been way back 120 years ago, notwithstanding today's observance of the same heavy engine's capacity to maintain its mighty power that it still drives on a daily basis after all these years!

Train riders have two options for the train trip.

The longer twenty-two miles, more scenic, much more enjoyable, and also more time-consuming run up Bald Knob—West Virginia's third highest mountain—is the highly recommended Bald Knob option. This prime, lengthier trip up Bald Knob includes an old-fashioned, box, picnic, tasty lunch. The Bald Knob trip may be the most adventure-filled train trip that any visitor can take, and still only travel its forty-four mile round-trip.

However, for those travelers restricted by time, the shorter trip to only Whitaker Station is only eight miles up and eight miles back, which takes two hours.

Whitaker Station is a cleared field with a **snack bar** available, while the primary purpose for Whitaker Station is for the engines to take on water. This stop is also used in the longer, four to five-hour Bald Knob trip.

Watching the train as it pulls up the steep incline to Bald Knob totally mesmerizes riders. Further up the mountain, the terrain becomes so steep as the engines chug around sharp curves. At those moments, it seems to cause the train to just "hang-on," by just trying to hug the mountains and avoid the sharp drop offs, over the sides opposite the mountains. It is in those instances that train travelers reach out of the windows just to watch the gearing literally huff and puff its way, while striving to climb higher, for most of the twenty-two miles. Visitors seem almost straining to hold on while snapping pictures, hanging on tightly as they keep one eye on the ambitious, churning train, and the other looking way down the constant supply of steep descents. At moments like these, most passengers abandon their seats, remain on their feet, and work to maintain their balance all the way to the top of Bald Knob. The only sounds apparent in thick, dense woods other than the chug-a-chugging are many riders shuffling their feet while holding onto their cameras recording the event! The thrill of listening all day to the train's steam whistle envelopes your heart and soul as if you were on a train to outer space! If you are planning a trip to Cass, all that can be offered is what a lifetime experience you are about to undertake!

The panoramic views from Bald Knob's tiptop become more embellished from the wooden, viewing stand overlook that extends out over the mountain's edge so that travelers can look straight down the 4,832 feet into the valley below. On cloudy or even stormy days, the dizzying view is most startling, especially when storms appear at sky levels quite a distance below the viewing stand. To view weather storms traversing, with heavy rain and sometimes rapidly moving cloud cover far below the present position of the viewing stand, is in itself an amazing work of nature. The opportunity to be outdoors and above a cloud and storm without riding in an airplane is seldom realized in life.

To summarize the day trip's most sterling adventures that heighten the excitement, during the trip up and back from Bald Knob, there are five key recollections and most memorable highlights. The first is where the switchback occurs. The second is at Whittaker Station, also the first water stop for the hardworking train engines, as passengers can jump off the train for a short period, buy snacks, and watch the action while taking pictures. The third occurs at the point where the conductor points out how much farther it will be to reach Bald Knob, while identifying the majestic mountain top from far away. The fourth is at a much-needed, train, water stop, preceding the period when the train begins chugging its hardest, through the very steepest terrain just before the arrival at Bald Knob. For a few short minutes, train riders can jump off, watch the engines take on water, and look over the steep, degressive ravine far down the mountain side. The fifth is the unique and stimulating views experienced at Bald Knob's top. The excitement doesn't end until after the train returns to Cass station, and the engineer wishes all a "good-bye" with several last heard blasts of the wondrous steam whistle.

Cass, WV, and especially the Cass Scenic Railroad State Park, have more than appreciably earned the highly esteemed AAA "GEMS" rating. This destination of the legendary steam engines and the most memorable train ride in the entire Country deserves inclusion on every traveler's "bucket list," as a "must-see" for American families. Much like my own experience as a youth, train travel, tours, and especially such a thrilling adventure that envelopes the Cass Scenic Railroad is most worthy of the utmost attention from families with youth, just to keep these aged, pleasurable, and historic activities in vogue.

To return to Lexington, just reverse the directions used to drive up to Cass from Lexington. As a review, those remain as follows: 1) from Cass take 66 east three miles to WV ST 28S, 2) next take 28S to Dunmore, WV four more miles, 3) then WV ST 92S to Frost, WV seven miles, 4) follow 92S to Minnehana, WV another ten miles, 5) then switch to WV ST 39 west into Virginia and Lexington fifty-five final miles, in this dazzling trip. That should take around two hours for the total one-way trip of seventy-nine miles, or a total of 158 miles on the day. Enjoy a good dinner and a good night's stay as preparation for a long next day of driving "homeward bound."

FRONT PORCH RESTAURANT, RICHBURG, SC

THE PALMS, LEXINGTON, VA

CHAPTER ELEVEN

DESTINATION
SAVANNAH, GA 421 MILES

NOTE: Now begins the end of this replication of the June 2019 trip, which originated in SW Florida. At this point, some optional or alternative destinations should be included, on the way home. There obviously must be a realization that individualized travelers' choices of attractions, destinations, and trip duration determine differentiated outcomes and options for each family's scheduled trips. As a result, plausible stops in Savannah and St. Augustine will be included in the itinerary covered in this guidebook. Options are many for engaging most all of the stops in a longer, perhaps two-week period. In short, it is most akin to humanity that all people are independently different and will do what, when, and where they prefer, can achieve, and want to drive to see for themselves. Also, it is expected that travelers will also originate trips from different points, as was covered in the "Introduction" section of this guidebook. With all those thoughts and expectations having been mentioned once again, completion of the book will resume with a "return home" itinerary.

The mileage from Lexington, VA, to St. Augustine, FL, is 605 miles. That may seem huge to some travelers, but considering that the driving is all on high speed interstates, and that only four large cities must be traversed, a full day of driving that attempts to escape those cities, during rush hour, could result in a tough but doable ten-hour driving day. The four cities that must be transgressed with various methods would include, in order: Charlotte, NC, (down the middle), Columbia, SC, (skirt), Savannah, GA (skirt), and Jacksonville, FL, (down the middle). By departing Lexington, VA, no later than 8:30 a.m., after a good breakfast, the prospective timing of noon for a luncheon stop could target Richburg, SC, which is about 202 miles. More on that recommendation will be addressed shortly.

Mileage from I-81S in Lexington, VA to its interchange with to I-77S, near Wytheville, VA is 100 miles. However, the most scenic part of the drive takes place another thirty miles past the interchange with I-77S, where I-77S passes under The Blue Ridge Parkway. At that point, I-77S takes a "nose dive"—very steep—descent through winding, weaving highway, while visitors try to simultaneously view one of the most beautiful, scenic panoramas on any U.S. highway. Concomitantly, as I-77S reaches the mountain's bottom, it also crosses the border into the "Tarheel State" of North Carolina. One of the most woody, relaxing rest stop areas awaits those in need at the entrance into North Carolina.

After the rest stop, there are only thirty-eight miles to anticipate the process of ambling through the usually congested Charlotte expressways—right through the heart of the city—while remaining on I-77S. Drivers must pay keen attention to highway directions to maintain the route on I-77S into northern South Carolina.

Front Porch Restaurant, Richburg, SC

Richburg, SC, is just inside South Carolina, whose motto is "The Palmetto State."

Richburg, SC, has one of the very best ever luncheon restaurants: **"The Front Porch."** This popular local restaurant has great home-cooked, southern foods, and great service, and is an easy stop—just off I-77 South at Exit 65, 3072, Lancaster Highway, on the left. Their hot roast beef, turkey, and meatloaf sandwiches, daily specials, and friendly demeanor are worth the effort.

To resume from either Charlotte or perhaps Richburg, the distance to the South Carolina state capital of Columbia, SC, and concomitantly the termination of I-77 is fifty-seven miles. Then proceed on I-26S south towards Charleston, SC, about halfway to I-95S another sixty-seven miles. Savannah,

GA is ninety-five miles further south on I-95S. Should a stopover await in Savannah, travelers should anticipate a cache of great experiences.

Savannah, with a population of 136,286, is situated just east twelve miles on I-16E from I-95. Another option is fifteen miles through Savannah on US 80E to the Atlantic Ocean—Tybee Island, a charming seaside resort.

Savannah, GA

There are only two options to see Savannah. One is by taking a self-guided, walking tour, and the other is to book a two-hour, guided, and narrated tour, with one of many qualified firms. We chose the Old Savannah Tours and were fascinated with the wealth of information gleaned from the tour guide. Savannah is steeped in history and architecture. Visiting Savannah exclusively in the spring provides an opportunity to enjoy the colorful beauty of the Azalea Festival.

RIVER STREET RESTAURANTS, SAVANNAH, GA

Savannah was founded in 1733, by James E. Oglethorpe and his settlers, who formed England's 13th and last colony. The founder and Colonel William Bull together pioneered a new and unique grid style for their new settlement. The format was labeled as a series of wards, in which commercial and residential buildings centered on a public square. Situated on a bluff overlooking the Savannah River, the future city burgeoned as a crossroads of trade between England and neighboring cities inland.

Two distinctly different economies combined to project Savannah into a fast-growing seaport: plantations, including tobacco and cotton, and seaport traffic that began as early as 1744.

Colonial General Robert Howe and his troops captured the city by surprise in 1778 and established a key Revolutionary War base against the British colonies, until 1782.

Savannah's new citizens supported the Colonial Army. "King Cotton" played a major role in Savannah's pivotal growth period of the 1800s. In 1862. Union forces in the Civil War captured rebel-held Fort Pulaski, just outside Savannah, on the Savannah River.

Union General William Tecumseh Sherman

overran Savannah two years later to continue his historic run from Chattanooga through Atlanta, to the key port of Savannah. In 1864, Confederate General William J. Hardee realized the futility of further combat and withdrew his troops away from Georgia, which saved Savannah from the same destruction suffered by Atlanta.

Although cotton became the big, economic, revitalization factor, after the Civil War, that surge extended only to around 1900 when cotton markets collapsed. That depression lasted until WW II. Still, the people reveled in what Sherman did to spare Savannah's destruction, since it maintained Savannah's uniqueness of squares, houses, and heritage—all key landmarks of Savannah still today. In 1955, seven women joined to save the historic Davenport House from demolition, as the city's fathers tried to tear down old, very historic buildings to further their movement to create a more modern skyline. This action formed the Historic Savannah Foundation, which became the nation's most successful urban restoration program. This endeavor succeeded through purchase of hundreds of properties and reselling them to other parties that supported restoration rather than modernization. Today

Savannah's plethora of historic buildings comprises a hallmark of the city. Lined with handsome townhouses, dressed up with fountains and historic statues, and beautified by oak trees and azaleas, Savannah is truly a charming city. The city is also distinctively identified by the existence of twenty-two of Oglethorpe's twenty-four original squares. Finally, the city cleaned up the Savannah River and tore down old, waterfront buildings, including many outdated, rundown, cotton, brokerage offices along Bay Street—all part of their urban development to revitalize Factor's Walk and River Street shops, restaurants, and nightspots.

Savannah is among the very few cities where there exists a combination of an enjoyable scenic walk and a plethora of excellent, seafood, dinner restaurants. River Street shops and well-rated restaurants are not far from most hotels. Included among the best of the list are: **Vic's On The River; Huey's; Tubby's Tank House; The Cotton Exchange;** and **The Shrimp Factory.** Also included for variety is **Spanky's Pizza Galley and Saloon.**

Fort Pulaski National Monument

Just fifteen miles east of Savannah, on US 80, Fort Pulaski National Monument offers a plethora of historical, keen insight into Savannah's participation in the Civil War. Located on both Cockspur and McQueens islands, at the mouth of the Savannah River, as the river empties into the Atlantic Ocean, the fort is on the eastern end of Cockspur island.

Both Fort George (1761-1776) and Fort Greene (1794-1804) preceded Fort Pulaski on the same site. Patriots on the American side disassembled the mostly wooden structure of Fort George in 1776, as the British naval fleet approached Savannah. Fort Greene, also constructed of wood, reached its end with a vicious hurricane in 1804.

In 1829, and continuing for a period of 18 years, the construction of Fort Pulaski took place, using over 25 million bricks to build the highly anticipated new fortress. United by an excellent, protective chain of forts running up and down the Atlantic coast, the new nation's most dependable bastille of defense from foreign invaders required stronger-built forts like Fort Pulaski. The new fort was designed as a huge, deviant pentagon-shaped fortress, which was surrounded by a moat that could

only be crossed with drawbridges. The long, inside halls are impressively identified with well-kilned brick archways. As a salute to those earlier constructors, the old fort even today survives as still a considerably well-built bastion. In fact Fort Pulaski still is considered as one of our nation's most visitor-friendly, for its true representation of our finest forts built during our country's earliest years.

The fort has earned the reputation as a key reason why U.S. firepower is still reputed as the strongest in the world, since this early fort experienced the very first display of the era's highly, militarily advanced use of rifled cannons. The Battle for Fort Pulaski took place in April of 1862, when it turned the Civil War in favor of the Union forces. The Union forces bombarded Fort Pulaski from nearby Tybee Island for thirty continuing hours, until the Confederate forces within the fort were forced to surrender. At the end of that key battle, the face of the fort most directly within the main line of fire had been demolished. The battle convinced military leaders that brick fortresses were no longer a match for the Union's most updated weaponry, represented by the rifled cannons, with their improved display of power, range, and accuracy.

Tybee Island

Tybee Island, just a half hour east on US 80, and located on the Atlantic Ocean, is a quiet, laid back, seaside resort island—quite apropos for a week's vacation. Its name came from Native American words for "salt." Tybee's beckoning three miles of sandy beaches, great restaurants, and combination of oceanside and ocean-front hotels make Tybee Island a dream relaxation spot.

TYBEE ISLAND

Tybee Island is so close to Savannah that time can be spent in both places.

Tybee Island Lighthouse

The Tybee Island Lighthouse is the oldest and tallest in the State of Georgia. It was constructed in the 1770s, due to its strategic location at the mouth of the Savannah River. As such, it became a historic defensive fortification in the 1880s.

Visitors to Savannah should ensure including a visit to this interesting and educational vestige of American wars of yesteryear. Also, the site is well-deserving of AAA's esteemed "GEM" rating, as a must-see, and inclusion on travelers' "bucket lists!"

From Savannah to St. Augustine is 184 miles. If possible, avoid Jacksonville, FL, at rush hour, as the route down I-95S south crosses (right down the middle), through the heart of Jacksonville. Jacksonville is the first city heading south into "The Sunshine State" of Florida.

VIEW OF AVILES STREET, ST. AUGUSTINE, FL

BRIDGE OF LIONS, MATANZAS RIVER, ST. AUGUSTINE, FL

CHAPTER TWELVE

DESTINATION
ST. AUGUSTINE, FL 184 MILES

St. Augustine, an all-time favorite, touristy city, is just forty-six miles south on I-95S from Jacksonville. The old-world charm of our nation's "Oldest City In America" is second to none in the USA! You can visit during the period of warmer weather, with sandy beaches and warm ocean current, or around the very special season of Christmas. St. Augustine's historical downtown is immersed in ribbons of beautiful holiday decorations and colorful lighting, at that celebrated time of year. Visit anytime, as St. Augustine will surely entertain you with its beauty, impressive historical sites, or tasteful and plentiful supply of restaurants. Shopping with two outlet malls and at other boutiques throughout the downtown are available also. As our Oldest City, you can imagine the long history of this scintillating city.

Certainly qualified for the title of our Nation's oldest and continuously inhabited settlement, in the contiguous United States, it was founded in 1565 by Spanish explorers. The name derives from the Spanish word for Saint Augustine or San Agustin in Spanish. The founder was a Spanish admiral named Pedro Menendez de Aviles, who subsequently became Florida's first governor. His ships, while loaded with settlers, supplies, and troops from Spain, had sited the area for days before coming ashore on August 28, 1565, which is the feast day of St. Augustine. Almost immediately, the city aspired to be the capital of Spanish Florida, which lasted for two hundred years. St. Augustine became the capital of British Florida for a twenty-year period from 1763 to 1783, until it was once again returned to Spain. In 1821, St. Augustine became the capital of the Florida Territory, after Spain had ceded Florida to the USA in 1819.

It is an interesting historical fact that the newly independent USA acquired East Florida from Spain, with an agreement to forgive Spanish debt to the USA of $5 million. In the same deal, Spain also gave up West Florida, and all claims to Oregon. When Andrew Jackson returned to Florida in 1821, he established a new territorial government, which led to massive migration from older, northern, and wealthier plantation settlements from Virginia, Georgia, and the Carolinas.

The territorial government moved the Florida capital to the present capital city of Tallahassee in 1824, as a result of a government issue to combine both East and West Florida. The choice of Tallahassee compromised the settlement of a dispute over the location of the territorial government, since Tallahassee resided halfway between then the two largest settlements of Pensacola to the West and St. Augustine to the East.

CASTILLO DE SAN MARCO

Soon Florida's population growth caused skirmishes between Native Americans and the new immigrants from the North. When local Creek and Miccosukee peoples tried to push the white settlers from their new settlements, the U.S. government attempted to relocate the Native Americans, resulting in a string of three Seminole Wars. The first Indian War occurred in 1823, when then Governor William Duval and James Gadsden tried to enforce the new Treaty of Moultrie Creek. This promoted displacing the Seminoles onto a four-million-acre reservation in central Florida. The second Seminole War, from 1835 to 1842, attempted once again to relocate the Seminole Tribe, but this time to a Creek Indian reservation west of the Mississippi River. Instead, former Revolutionary War General Francis Marion changed the name of St. Augustine's Fort Castillo de San Marcos to Fort Marion and used the fort to hold the Seminole prisoners.

By 1840, the population passed 50,000 people, half of which were made up of enslaved African Americans. In 1845, Florida entered statehood. When the Confederacy was created in 1861, Florida capitulated as a Confederate State, which lasted for only fourteen months, primarily because Florida was poorly defended, during the Union's blockade of the St. Augustine ports. The blockade gained control of Florida, in 1862, which the Union maintained through the end of the Civil War. However, the Civil War caused an economic depression, which resulted in the departure of much of the Florida population.

The Standard Oil Company's co-founders were John D. Rockefeller and Henry Flagler. Flagler became Florida's savior when he spent the winter of 1883, in St. Augustine.

Flagler was enamored with St. Augustine and it led him to utilize the term of "his most charming city." He resolutely dismissed the established hotels and transportation system as inadequate, so he decided to make improvements and upgrades. His goal was to turn St. Augustine into a wealthy, winter resort. To accomplish that goal, he bought several shoreline railroads, which he combined in 1885 into the new Florida East Coast Railway. He also constructed a bridge over the St. Johns River in 1888, which promptly led to a revitalized economy since the new bridge opened up travel from the North. In 1887, he built two new hotels: the 450-room Hotel Ponce de Leon, and the 250-room Hotel Alcazar. These additions gave St. Augustine a new and noticeable skyline. In addition, he hired a popular architectural firm to mold the buildings into the present Moorish Revival style, which graces the city today. All these upgrades turned the city into a Winter resort overnight.

However, Flagler seemed to outdo himself when, in the early 1900s he extended his new railroad to the southern Florida cities of West Palm Beach and Miami. This extension resulted in shifting the most popular Winter retreats further South than St. Augustine, simply because the Winters in extreme southern Florida are warmer and somewhat more pleasant. Still, St. Augustine enjoyed a stabilized economy from a reduced amount of winter tourism, especially from families who drove their cars from up North, and disdained the extra 200 miles to the southern Florida resorts.

The city survived the 1963 Civil Rights movement sit-ins, protests, and violence, which included the only arrest of the Reverend Martin Luther King, the violent attacks by the Ku Klux Klan, and resultant poor national publicity. Since the late 1800s, St. Augustine has become a preferential historical destination, which it still claims—and rightfully so—today.

New visitors would perhaps gain their best introduction to the city by booking a guided tour which envelopes all the historical attractions. Recommended is the Old Town Trolley, which both welcomed and introduced us to St. Augustine when we decided to build a new home near the city, in late 2017.

The plentiful supply of comfortable hotels and often favorite restaurants out on St. Augustine Beach's A1A oceanfront drive almost guarantees a fun stay and a resting and relaxing experience.

Perhaps the two most popular St. Augustine restaurants include the **Sunset Grille** at 421 A1A Beach Blvd., and the **Raintree Restaurant** on San Marco Blvd., adjacent to the Historic District. The fresh grouper dinner at Sunset Grille and the Cappellini Pomodoro at the Raintree are both scrumptious and often favorites! St. Augustine also has a plentiful supply of good hotels, which are seemingly clustered in three specific areas: the beach and A1A, the downtown historic district, and the State Road 16 intersection with I-95.

St. Augustine was our June 2019 wonderful trip's last overnight stop, albeit the 345 mile drive home to SW Florida. We had travelled a total of 2,992 miles through eight states, and experienced twenty attractions in eleven full days; we thoroughly enjoyed the entire trip.

Many stops comprised our second and third visits over a period of fifty-five years of marriage. We started traveling with our three children, then later resumed our travels as new empty nesters, and recently over the past score of years, since 2001, as retired seniors. For the record, we have experienced every destination, attraction, and experience detailed in this guidebook. We are hopeful of continuing our travels in the near future. Since we have toured the United States almost completely, we are now targeting second and third visits to those destinations deemed our most memorable favorites. Also, we plan to tour the Canadian Maritime Provinces for the first time.

Over the several years that we have lived in SW Florida, we usually have stayed overnight in St. Augustine, at various hotels, though majorly at the Hilton Garden Inn out on beautiful A1A, which is a half block stroll from the beaches of the Atlantic Ocean. Since the drive home is about five hours or so, but highly congested through Orlando, we have made an unwavering habit of rising early, and driving about fifty miles to Ormond Beach, FL, down I-95 south.

Well advertised with billboards along the extremely busy expressway, the **Ormond Beach Cracker Barrel** offers a great, hot, and home-cooked breakfast, as well as a stop for other reasons, including an adjacent, favorite of a **Dunkin Donuts** for a take out coffee. The excellent **Cracker Barrel** restaurant is located at 125 Interchange Road, just off I-95, and a quick left into the restaurant's drive. Their phone is: 386-673-5400.

Please note that this travel guidebook entails over thirty interesting, enjoyable, and educational destinations. Although we have visited and experienced all thirty travel stops, some many times, this trip did not include either Savannah's or St. Augustine's listed attractions, other than the excellent St. Augustine restaurant on A1A—the **Sunset Grill,** as well as the nearby Hilton Garden Inn.

Happy Travels!

The End!

www.ingramcontent.com/pod-product-compliance
Lightning Source LLC
LaVergne TN
LVHW052346100826
845147LV00012B/760

9781735252551